THE SOLAR

COASTER

THE SOLAR INDUSTRY'S ULTIMATE PLAYBOOK

ANNA COVERT

DEDICATION

To my daughter Emma,

I'm so proud to be your mother. Your heart is magic, and your smile lights up every room. You've told me you want to be a singer, a designer—maybe both—and I believe you can be anything.

You are my reason.

When I think about the future, I see you—bright, bold, and full of possibility. Your dreams remind me why hope matters, why action matters. This book is my promise: I gave it everything I had, for you and the world you'll help shape.

Never stop manifesting what makes your heart sing. And never let anyone tell you there's no hope.

Love always,
Mom

TABLE OF CONTENTS

INTRODUCTION

The gates swing open, and the air is alive with the smell of buttery popcorn and freshly paved asphalt. The crowd surges forward, a kaleidoscope of families with wide-eyed kids, thrill-seekers itching for that adrenaline hit, and couples sneaking in hand-holding and stolen kisses.

From gravity-defying loops to haunted house horrors, from overpriced souvenirs to unexpected rain showers, a trip to the park is never just about the rides—it's about the entire journey. Some leave exhilarated, others a little queasy, but no one forgets the highs and lows they encountered along the way.

The same is true when you take a trip on what we solar diehards refer to as "The Solar Coaster," because the industry attracts people from far and wide, all with a common goal— save the planet and make a penny or two in the process. The playful name points to the peaks and valleys that those in the field often find themselves flung into, but when uttered among comrades, it's always met with a sly smile, despite the truth that it reveals about the industry. And just like with any theme park ride, you might eagerly wait in line thinking it's all thrills—only to find yourself caught off guard by some unexpected twists and turns. It's not always smooth sailing, and at times, it can leave you feeling a little queasy.

You might ask yourself, "Why get on at all?" For some adrenaline junkies, it's the thirst for adventure and the possibility of reaching new heights: for others, it's the fear of missing out, but one thing is for sure, it's not for everyone. Similarly, the solar industry is not for the faint of heart, but for those who can stomach it, they'll tell you that it has more ups than downs, and the excitement is unreal.

This book comes at a pivotal moment in solar's evolution. When I first started writing, SunPower—once considered the gold standard in American solar—had just filed for Chapter 11 bankruptcy. Today, as I finalize this manuscript, that same brand is already charting a comeback. If that's not the solar coaster in real time, I don't know what is.

Things move fast in this industry. The highs are thrilling. The lows are humbling. But even in the darkest moments, the light finds a way through.

Just as I finish these pages, a new jolt hits the industry: the ITC step-down bill, unofficially known as the "One Big Beautiful Bill," was signed into law by President Trump on July 4, 2025. It officially sunsets the 30% Residential Clean Energy (ITC) tax credit on December 31, 2025, with no phase-down or extension—marking a seismic shift for residential solar. Commercial credits will remain in place a bit longer, but the writing is on the wall. These incentives have powered a decade of unprecedented adoption, helping both families and businesses take control of their energy bills, stay resilient during outages, and support local jobs.

This is the reality of solar: record growth one year, mass layoffs the next. One administration accelerates progress, the next slams the brakes. And through it all, the industry keeps moving—innovating, adapting, lighting the way.

What I've learned is this: no matter what's happening in boardrooms or on Capitol Hill, the people in this industry are resilient. That's who this book is for.

Whether you're a solar veteran or just getting started, I wrote *The Solar Coaster* to help you navigate the chaos with clarity, creativity, and confidence—to make smarter decisions, recover faster from setbacks, and stay focused on your mission, even when the market whiplashes.

Because the future of solar will belong to those who evolve. Rapid consolidation, financial volatility, and constant tech breakthroughs are reshaping the game. In solar, nothing stays the same for long. And no one—not even the giants—is immune to the ride.

But with the right mindset, you can do more than survive it. You can rise with it.

This book is your playbook for exactly that—packed with insights, hard-won lessons, and strategies that work. Use it to adapt faster, lead smarter, and build something that lasts—no matter what the solar coaster throws your way.

Why Trust Anna-lytics?

I officially became a solar business owner twice: the first time briefly in 2020 and once again in 2024 with the launch of a solar sales organization under Powur. But I was no novice. I had spent 10 years developing winning strategies to market and sell solar products before I decided to expand from marketing strategist to solar entrepreneur. And almost immediately, I discovered what I knew—and what I needed to know.

Like many solar veterans, I got my start at SunPower. At one point, I owned two of the twelve approved partner businesses eligible for manufacturer credits. My advertising agency, Covert Communication, and direct mail company, Aerial Impacts, were both on the list. This meant that as dealers installed SunPower panels, they built up dealer credits—better known as DPF funds—which they could use on approved marketing services (like mine) or manufacturer-backed products such as appointments, design software, cell break kits, and company swag (shirts, cups, hats, even coloring books!).

This opportunity allowed me to work with hundreds of dealers nationwide, spanning residential and commercial solar companies—including sales-only operations, installation-only businesses, and hybrid companies that both sold and installed systems. During COVID, I was fortunate to become a SunPower vendor for high-end technology services. My company was directly paid by the manufacturer to provide API integrations between top dealer CRMs (customer relationship management systems) and the SunPower portal. While many vendors could map leads one way (from SunPower to a dealer's CRM), very few could successfully map data back.

And like many, I was in the thick of the solar meltdown—but luckily, I had already diversified before SunPower officially shut down its dealer program.

Over the past decade, I've established myself as a trusted expert in the solar industry by leading innovative marketing and tech initiatives across the board. I built Panasonic's first solar + storage calculator, launched *Solar Wizard* (now the #1 solar plugin in the world), developed the leads program for REC Group, and consulted with major brands like SolarEdge and Generac. I became the first approved marketing provider for Maxeon's dealer program and worked as a creative vendor for Complete Solar, which now carries the name SunPower by Complete Solar... and the list goes on.

Not only that, but I have personally sold hundreds of kilowatts of solar—powering dozens of homes—and have built a reputation as an industry leader in solar marketing, sales, technology, and business strategy. I've watched companies rise and fall, but what I'm most proud of is helping businesses stay afloat and pivot when the industry demanded it.

What You'll Learn in the Pages Ahead
In Chapters 1 and 2, we begin with the lifeblood of any solar business— leads. We'll explore both organic and paid approaches. Here's a quick peek at what's ahead.

Chapter 1: Leads, Baby!
We'll dive into grassroots strategies that work—referrals, incentives, rebates, reputation-building, breakout PR, events, direct mail, and door knocking that generate high-quality solar leads.

Chapter 2: Paid Lead Programs
Then we'll tackle the wild world of paid leads—dealer networks, manufacturer programs, co-branded funnels, and third-party marketplaces. You'll learn how to evaluate lead sources, negotiate fair terms, and avoid the common traps that drain your resources.

Chapter 3: Solar Sales Strategies—The Good, The Bad, and The Super Shady
With leads flowing in, it's time to sell. This chapter breaks down which techniques close deals today—from building trust and framing value to spotting red flags and staying compliant. You'll also get the real story on sales models used across the industry—for better or worse.

Chapter 4: The Sweet Spot—Hybrid Sales & the Psychology of Persuasion
Here we go deep on behavioral science-backed sales strategies, including how to build urgency, avoid common traps, and leverage the Setter/Closer model to turn interest into signed contracts.

Chapter 5: Building the Super Nova Team
Thriving solar teams aren't winging it. We'll break down how role separation, clear systems, and smart leadership fuel scalable success.

Chapter 6: A Sunsational Installation Experience
From site survey to PTO, this chapter walks through the full installation process. More importantly, it shows how to turn installs into reviews, referrals, and recurring revenue through post-sale support and operations & maintenance (O&M) services.

Chapter 7: Scaling Your Business—Tales from the Street
Here's where it gets juicy. You'll hear real stories from the field—case studies from companies that didn't just survive the solar coaster…they scaled it. Learn how these leaders diversified, pivoted, and stayed ahead of the curve.

Chapter 8: Policy and Beyond
We wrap it all up by zooming out. From tax credits to carbon markets, this chapter explores how policy, the Environmental Social Governance (ESG) framework, and financing are shaping the future of solar—and how you can position your business to thrive no matter what happens next. You'll find case studies on creative financing models that help

companies close deals with or without incentives, plus strategies for navigating uncertainty when policies shift. Tax credits may come and go, but those who innovate will always ride the storm.

By the end, you'll be equipped to build trust, convert leads, and elevate your solar business at every stage of the customer journey.

And as always, we'll keep coming back to one key theme- While solar companies may want to do it all, should they? Knowing your strengths—and where to bring in help—can be the difference between burnout and building a business that thrives.

Let me be your solar coaster ringmaster, guiding you through the twists, turns, and opportunities of this dynamic industry. And along the way, I'll be sharing real stories, lessons, and interviews with industry leaders who've lived it, learned from it, and are lighting the path forward.

You might find yourself underlining, scribbling in the margins, or highlighting like it's an Olympic sport (no shame—I'm right there with you). Just know you don't have to capture everything in the moment. There's a full treasure trove of resources online, including extended interviews with all the experts featured in the book and beyond. Explore as much (or as little) as you like, whenever you're ready to dive deeper.

Get ready—because this ride is just getting started.

CHAPTER ONE:

LEADS, BABY!

> *"Organic leads are gold. Service, community, and reputation—that's what drives long-term opportunity."*
>
> — Kelley Barber, Solar Sales & Marketing leader since 2007

Selling solar has been one of the most rewarding—and eye-opening—experiences of my career. It's one of the few industries where everyone truly wins: the homeowner, the salesperson, the installer, and yes, the planet. That's what makes it so compelling and why the high is hard to beat. But even in the short time I've been in the game, I've watched things shift fast.

When I started, it felt like the opportunity was endless. Leads were flowing, homeowners were eager, and the momentum was electric. But lately? The terrain feels different. Lead generation has slowed. Consumer skepticism is higher. And everywhere I turn, new solar companies are popping up, all competing for a pool of prospects that suddenly feels a lot smaller.

You might be feeling it too: lead quality is down, costs are up, and conversions are harder to win. So, what's going on?

Before we dive into the different types of leads—whether you're self-generating, buying, or building through referral networks—there's something even more important to address.

No matter where your leads come from, your business needs to understand the customer journey and communicate one critical message at every step: "Why you?"

Because in a crowded market, clarity wins.

What Kind of Dealer Are You?

It might sound obvious, but I speak with clients daily who still struggle to define their niche. Sure, you *can* try to do it all—but should you?

Knowing your core business type provides the foundation—your North Star—for building the right marketing strategy and operational focus.

While solar veterans may already be familiar with these roles, this book is written for both seasoned professionals and newcomers alike. So, before we go any further, let's quickly break it down and help you figure out where you fit. Knowing your role is the first step to playing it well.

Understanding the Core Business Models in Solar

Before you build a lead strategy, it's critical to understand the business model you're operating under. Each model comes with different responsibilities, margins, and growth opportunities—and your lead generation strategy should align accordingly.

Here's a breakdown of the four main types of solar organizations:

Company Types

Installers: Installers are responsible for the entire solar installation process, including design, permitting, installation, and sometimes maintenance of both their own systems and orphaned systems installed by others.

Installers with Sales Teams: These companies offer a full-service solution, managing both sales and operations. They have an internal sales team that secures contracts and an installation team that takes over the project to ensure completion.

Sellers: These organizations focus solely on sales and do not handle installations themselves. Instead, they partner with EPCs (Engineering, Procurement, and Construction) to coordinate the installation process.

When it comes to solar sales compensation, how your deals are priced plays a significant role in your earning potential—and in how transparently your team can operate.

The most common commission structures include:

- Flat commissions for appointments booked, demos completed, or deals closed
    - Per-appointment (demo run) commission- Typically, $50–$100
    - Per-closed deal commission- Either a flat rate or a percentage of the total sale
- System size-based commissions: Calculated by price per watt
    - Redline Example: For a 30 kW system → 30 × 1,000 × $0.10 = $3,000
    - In a redline model, you earn the difference between a set base price and your sale price—simple math with big earning potential, but it can lead to inconsistent pricing and trust issues.
- Price-based commission: Let's say you sell a 10 kW system for $45,000.
    - Powur Example: The cost of goods sold (COGS) is $30,000, leaving a $15,000 profit margin (70%) for the salesman and $4,500 (30%) going to Powur, the EPC.

o   In a COGS model, commissions are based on profit after actual job costs, promoting transparency, ethical pricing, and team alignment—though it may limit the upside on certain deals and requires more backend clarity.

EPC (Engineering, Procurement, and Construction) Organizations: EPCs build scalable networks of installers and sales partners, offering full-service turnkey solutions for market expansion. Companies like Powur, Axia by Qcells, Thryve, and SunPower by Complete Solar fill this role—streamlining operations and marketing to both sides of the industry to enable efficient growth.

This model is ideal for companies that want to stay focused on their core strength—whether that's selling or installing—while still participating in broader growth opportunities.

Each model has its own pros and cons. As we move into the next section on lead generation, keep your business structure in mind. Your role directly influences how you generate, qualify, and convert leads—and ultimately, how you scale.

Once you know what kind of dealer you are and how your business is structured, it's time to turn outward—toward your customers. Regardless of whether you're generating your own leads, buying them, or relying on referrals, your success will ultimately come down to this: how well you guide potential customers through their buying journey. In a market that's more competitive—and more skeptical—than ever, understanding this journey is no longer optional. It's essential.

What is the Customer Journey?

In solar—just like in any industry—the goal is to move potential customers through four key stages: Awareness, Consideration, Intent, and Action. The larger the investment, the longer this cycle typically takes. A commercial solar installation, for example, will require far more touchpoints and decision-making time than upselling a battery to an existing residential solar customer.

But here's the key: The customer journey isn't a straight line; it's fluid. Let's simplify it into three parts.

1. Marketing generates awareness and consideration.

2. Sales moves the customer from intent to action.

3. Installation delivers the experience that fulfills the promise.

Throughout this journey, our job as solar professionals is to educate, build trust, and nurture—before, during, and after the sale.

On the front end, the solar customer journey follows some predictable patterns. Using data from Quantcast (a global platform with over 100 million website pixels), we know the typical residential solar customer spends 28–32 days from first site visit to requesting quotes from 2–3 companies. In maturing markets, that number is stretching to 35–40 days, likely due to consumer fatigue and oversaturation.

Why the delay?

Consumers today are often overwhelmed. Many use "free solar estimator" tools on third-party sites like Solar Reviews or others, but what they don't realize is that these sites sell and resell their information to multiple lead buyers. That means that, within hours, they're bombarded by a dozen or more calls, texts, and emails. It's aggressive. It's invasive. And for many consumers, it's the moment they shut down and drop out of the market entirely.

Lead Fatigue Is Real—And It's Getting Worse

While lead programs are the backbone of many solar companies, the rise in digital fraud, third-party reselling, and regulatory uncertainty has complicated things. As someone who's run paid media campaigns, consulted with national lead providers, and launched my own lead gen tools, I can tell you that not all leads are created equal.

The reality? Estimates show that 35-45% of all web traffic today is fake[1], driven by bots, click farms, and bad actors. On top of that, 55-60% of programmatic ads are served on low-performing or low-quality sites— the kind that bait you with headlines like *"Lose 20 Pounds Eating Avocados"* only to bombard you with pop-ups the moment you land. Sure, the impressions are there—but did anyone *really see* your message? Nope.

Pair that with 10-12% of impressions served in irrelevant geographies and another 5-8% shown to completely mismatched audiences[2], and it's easy to see why so many solar companies feel like they're burning cash— wasting a significant portion of their ad spend and form fills on traffic that will never convert.

A (Brief) Regulatory Rollercoaster

In late 2024, the FCC approved the One-to-One Consent Rule, requiring consumers to explicitly opt-in to the exact company they wanted to be contacted by—effectively banning the shady practice of mass lead reselling.

I was thrilled. It was a long-overdue step toward transparency and consumer trust. But the celebration didn't last.

Just days before implementation, the rule was delayed. And then, on January 24, 2025, the U.S. Court of Appeals struck it down, ruling that the FCC had overstepped its authority. Now, with no enforcement in place, the reselling frenzy is worse than ever. Some companies are even using AI-curated homeowner lists—with no valid opt-in whatsoever.

This means what you'll learn in the following chapters is more critical than ever.

---

1 https://www.globenewswire.com/news-release/2025/05/29/3090666/0/en/Pixalate-Releases-Q1-2025-Global-Connected-TV-CTV-Ad-Supply-Chain-Trends-Reports-Open-Programmatic-Ad-Spend-Rises-10-YoY-to-5-Billion-Ad-Fraud-IVT-Hits-18.html

https://www.wsj.com/business/media/efforts-to-weed-out-fake-users-for-online-advertisers-fall-short-0a5ec1a6

2 https://clicksambo.com/en/blog-detail/click-fraud-in-2025-alarming-statistics

Lead Management Best Practices (That Most Ignore)

I dive deep into digital ads and (CRM lead management best practices) in the Amazon best-selling book *The Covert Code—Mastering the Art of Digital Marketing*, which was published by Forbes Books June 18th, 2024 so I won't rehash that here. But know this: the same principles apply to all lead sources, whether you buy them or generate them in-house.

To compete in this environment:

- **Track lead quality continuously.** Never "set and forget." Just because a source worked yesterday doesn't mean it will work tomorrow. Lead performance is influenced by a wide range of variables—seasonality, market saturation, shifting consumer behavior, even the weather. Add to those internal factors like team changes, sales training gaps, or personal challenges affecting your setters and closers, and it's clear: lead quality is a moving target that demands ongoing attention.

- **Speed-to-lead matters.** Engage fast—or someone else will.

- **Give your providers quality feedback.** Help optimize the campaigns you're paying for or referral networks you're nurturing.

- **Respect opt-out and DND (Do Not Disturb) rules.** Nurturing should last for well over 90 days (I personally go up to a full year) but must be done ethically.

You must have a well-designed website, proper tracking, smart remarketing, and a solid CRM in place. Spending money on marketing without this infrastructure is just bad business. Once a lead engages, they're conducting their own audit. They're Googling your business, checking reviews, clicking through your site, and judging your credibility before they ever attend the meeting. If your digital presence doesn't build confidence, you've likely lost the sale before it even starts.

So, How Do You Win the Customer?

It starts with what they see, hear, and experience when they land on your site.

From all the solar websites the agency has managed, we've noticed that the average visit time on a residential solar site is 4–5 minutes before a conversion. For commercial solar, that number jumps to 8–11 minutes. That time is your window to earn trust, showcase value, and build confidence.

The modern buyer scrolls first and reads second. Your content must be clear, credible, and conversion focused.

How to Establish Authority & Build Consumer Confidence

To earn trust in an oversaturated market, you need more than a slick website. You need proof and authenticity.

Start with clear, value-driven messaging across your website, marketing, and outreach. Speak directly to your audience and include engagement opportunities that offer something meaningful in exchange for their time and information—like a downloadable white paper, an instant quote, system size estimate, or a 3D model of their home with solar. Give before you ask.

But don't stop there. Today's consumers crave real connection. That means sharing your company's story, your mission, and why you're in this business in the first place. Whether it's your passion for sustainability, desire to build a better future for your family, or commitment to serving your local community—your "why" can be one of your most powerful marketing tools. People connect with people, not just products and solutions.

Here are the essential trust signals every solar company should be showcasing:

- **Third-party verified reviews** (Google, BBB, Best Company, Yelp, etc.)
- **Video testimonials** are still the most powerful trust-builder.
- **Years in business & leadership credentials**

- **Badges & certifications** that show you're the real deal:
  - o REC Gold Installer, Maxeon Preferred Partner, Tesla Authorized Dealer
  - o NABCEP® Certification
  - o State recognitions like NYSERDA or CALSSA, SEIA membership
  - o Local awards from Nextdoor, regional media, or your local chamber of commerce

These trust signals are massively underrated—but they carry serious weight. They're the silent validators that tell the customer that you're the right choice. Now I think it goes without saying that authority and trust don't just live on your website. You need to put them in front of your audience—early, often, and across multiple channels. One of the most effective ways to do that? Direct mail.

In a sea of emails, ads, and cold calls, a well-crafted piece of mail stands out. It's personal and tangible, and when done right, it plants the seed of trust before the customer ever picks up the phone or clicks a link. Let's start there: how to use direct mail to generate quality organic leads—and then layer in the other channels that will keep your pipeline full!

Direct Mail is Making a Comeback

Over the past decade, direct mail lost ground as businesses flocked to faster, cheaper outreach methods like email, text, and call centers. The rise of digital search and programmatic ads made direct mail seem outdated—especially for companies chasing instant, trackable lead sources.

But what started as a seemingly more affordable digital strategy has shifted. In many cases, the economics have flipped. Solar-related keywords now often cost $5 to $60+ per click. And even if every click is from a real person, that's a hefty price to pay without knowing whether it's an actual homeowner (and dare we add to our list of demands...qualified!).

My first deep dive into direct mail for solar began with a product I launched in September 2019 called Aerial Impacts. The concept was the brainchild of Ellsworth Corum III[3] and was simple but powerful:

1. Curate high-quality homeowner data—removing rental properties, multi-family dwellings, and homes owned by trusts. One requirement for this campaign to be cost-effective was a minimum

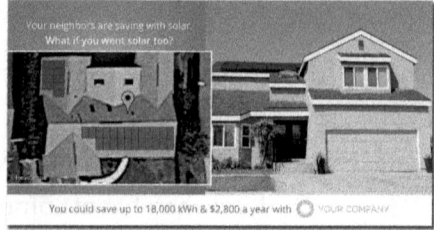

Aerial Impacts

send of 3,000 mailers. To achieve this, we needed to acquire at least 4,500 records (depending on market saturation) to account for homes with existing systems—something that's becoming more complex as Google Earth data can often be several years out of date in certain locations.

2. Use Helioscope (now Aurora or OpenSolar) for automated solar designs—leveraging an offshore team to pre-design systems based on predefined technology solutions (e.g., SunPower 360s) and local regulations; for example, in Florida any system over 11.5 kW requires a special permit, so we designed systems to be under that size.

3. Send high-impact variable print mailers—beautiful 5.5 x 11 postcards featuring aerial imagery of the recipient's home with a solar design overlay, a personalized savings estimate, and a clear call to action.

Each custom mailer cost $1.75–$2 to produce and send, and we saw an impressive 2–5% response rate from a single mailing! SunPower and

---

3 Watch the podcast with Ellsworth Corum III on annacovert.com

Panasonic quickly took notice, approving Aerial Impacts for use in their exclusive dealer programs—momentum was building.

Then COVID hit, and response rates plummeted. To counteract this, we tested a combo mailer approach:

- Step 1: Send a bulk, non-personalized warm-up mailer letting homeowners know a custom solar design was on its way, dropping the cost of the first mailer to around $0.55.

- Step 2: Follow up with the customized Aerial Impacts card.

This approach yielded more typical direct mail results—around a 0.5% to 2% response rate after two drops. But as demand tapered off, many companies turned to Google Ads, which were proving more cost-effective at the time. This shift also aligned with changing homeowner behavior, as the market moved rapidly from in-home appointments to virtual sales.

> *"When the pandemic hit, no one wanted to open their doors. But with low interest rates, people stuck at home, and extra cash to spend, it was the perfect storm for virtual sales."*
>
> – Greg Field, PGT Solar Solutions

The Shift to EDDM – Every Door Direct Mail

Rather than targeting just 3,000 carefully selected homes at a higher cost per piece, we opted for scale. Rising costs and limitations with minimum order sizes and outdated aerial imagery pushed us to pivot to EDDM (Every Door Direct Mail)—a more budget-friendly approach that allowed us to:

- Cherry-pick postal routes using USPS data.

- Qualify for bulk mailing discounts.

- Mail to every home on the route for as little as $0.17 per piece.

With just 2–3 mail drops, we achieved a 1.5% conversion rate—a solid result for top-of-funnel awareness. However, EDDM has its limitations, particularly for brands without strong local presence. Homeowners were far more likely to engage when they also saw branded solar trucks, yard signs, and door-to-door reps reinforcing the message. Integrating door knockers into the direct mail strategy helped create those layered, repeated impressions that build familiarity and trust.

What many companies miss is that direct mail is just the beginning—it's top-of-funnel advertising. Once that postcard lands in a homeowner's hands, the next steps are consideration and intent—which almost always lead them to search online. That's where things fall apart for many solar companies. If your website is outdated, lacks credibility signals (like reviews, trust badges, or financing options), or isn't built with a clear conversion path, you're warming up the lead just to hand them off to a competitor who looks better.

To close the loop, your mailer should include a scannable QR code that drives traffic directly into a well-designed funnel—whether that's a landing page built around a promo or an interactive quote tool. The site must be fast, mobile-optimized, and designed to move users from curious to converted.

While QR code scams have become more common (the FTC issued a consumer alert on this trend in 2024[4]), they remain a highly effective tool when used with clear branding and trust signals. The goal is to make it obvious to the homeowner who is sending them the mail and why they should feel confident scanning your code.

The best-performing direct mail campaigns incorporate:

- **A clear call to action** – drive urgency with a compelling offer.

---

4 Federal Trade Commission, Consumer Alert on QR Code Scams, 2024

- **Behavioral marketing principles** – leverage scarcity, social proof, and loss aversion (we'll dive deeper into these concepts in Chapter 4).

- **Value-driven incentives** – for example, "Get a free solar attic fan with installation" or a limited-time rebate offer.

- **Trackable QR codes** – branded and designed to drive instant engagement with a clear lead form or scheduler.

- **Conversion-optimized website funnels** – guide prospects toward action with seamless, intentional design.

Mail gets you in the door. The rest of your funnel determines whether you stay in the running.

What's Next in Direct Mail?

Direct mail is evolving. Today, it's no longer about mass printing and hoping someone bites—it's about personalization, timing, and integration. With CRM-based variable printing, we can now trigger mailers that are tailored to each homeowner's journey, reinforcing the right message at the right time.

But this shift didn't come out of nowhere. For me, it started with one frustrating experience on a hot afternoon in Waipahu—one that changed the way I thought about solar sales forever.

The Birth of Solar Assault: A Smarter Approach to Selling Solar

It was a hot day in Oahu, and I was eager to meet Gabriel Chong, Head Engineer for Sunspear Energy, the local dealer I was selling solar for (and an agency advertising client). Our appointment was at a home in Waipahu and generated from SunPower. As I pulled up, Gabe arrived at the same time, but instead of enthusiasm, he sighed, "Oh no, I've been here before."

I didn't see the problem yet—I was still new to solar sales. Gabe explained, "These homeowners never go solar. Every couple of years, they review options but never pull the trigger. Just a gigantic waste of time."

I wasn't convinced. They hadn't had ME sell them solar yet, right? Cocky? Absolutely—but my numbers backed it up. My in-person close rate was 85%, and my virtual close rate sat at 55-60%—stats worth bragging about.

Inside, I met the typical Hawaii extended family—four generations under one roof, from crawling babies to Grandma in her wheelchair on oxygen. Their electric bill was $650 per month and growing. I launched into my pitch: company story, superior panel technology, warranties, and installation process. They needed financing, so we structured a Sunnova 25-year loan at 0.99%. Grandma was instantly approved. And the system would include three Powerwalls and an 18 kW array of REC panels—cutting their bill in half and protecting them from rising utility rates.

Slam dunk, right? Wrong. They didn't sign. We left.

The Follow-Up Game

Being relentless, I refused to accept this poor decision-making. I stayed top-of-mind by sending some fun cartoons that resonated with the Sunday comics section every Friday afternoon—a strategy I used with all my leads. These broke through the noise of typical text messages, appealing to homeowners by triggering nostalgia and visual engagement.

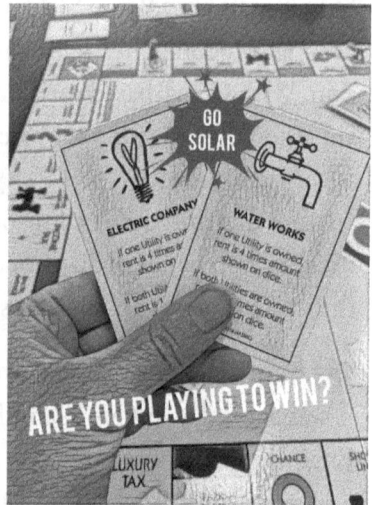

Four months later, I got the call. "You're the only rep still reaching out—why don't you come back?" I booked the appointment, already counting my commission (big mistake!).

Back at their kitchen table, the process repeated in the same manner, it was right out of Groundhog Day. They were approved and ready to save immediately. But again—crickets.

Frustrated, I asked, "I don't understand, what's your hesitation?"

The homeowner looked at me and said, "What do we do in 25 years?"

Without thinking, I blurted out, "You'll be dead, and your kids will have gone to college with the money you saved."

Not my best moment.

The Turning Point

Driving home, licking my wounds and replaying the appointment over in my head, I had an epiphany: this wasn't about logic, numbers, or long-term savings. It wasn't even about solar.

The pitch was sound. The offer was strong. The financing was unbeatable. But I was selling the wrong story.

Most solar reps—including me at the time—were leaning on the same worn-out lines: *"What if you could lock in a guaranteed 15% return for 25 years?"*

But here's the truth: most homeowners aren't thinking in decades. They're not investing in the stock market. They're living paycheck to paycheck, juggling groceries, gas, and electric bills. They're not planning for year 25—they're just trying to survive next month.

I realized: They didn't need future savings. They needed an immediate, tangible reward.

So, I asked myself: What if, instead of pitching a 25-year savings plan, I told them, 'If I gave you a Visa gift card for $200 every month, would that change your life?'

Because let's be real—$200/month means groceries. It means saving up for new tires. It means a much-deserved family vacation. It means breathing room. And that hits differently than abstract financial projections.

That's when I had the idea that would evolve into the *Coulda, Shoulda Campaign*—a way to send homeowners visual, physical reminders that could touch on what they were missing every single month they didn't go solar.

The idea was simple: instead of letting the deal die, we'd keep following up—not with generic messages, but with personalized mailers showing them what key bite-sized milestones of lost savings actually looked like in their everyday life.

1. $250: Grocery bags filled with food.

2. $500: A cozy dinner-for-two setup at a restaurant.

3. $750: New car tires.

4. $1,000: A washing machine or household appliance.

5. $1,500: A laptop for work or school.

6. $2,000: A weekend family getaway.

7. $2,500: A stylish new sofa or living room set.

8. $3,000: Utility bills marked "Paid"

9. $3,500: A family outing, such as tickets to a theme park.

10. $4,000: A used car in good condition.

11. $5,000: A home renovation scene and final messaging.

And that one idea turned into *Solar Assault*—a behavioral marketing engine built on timing, relevance, and a whole lot of regret.

Today: Solar Assault in Action

Now, we use CRM triggers to automate direct mail—personalized, timely, and cost-effective. This works because the homeowner is already in the database and has started their journey. It's not cold; it's tepid or hot depending on the lead source and where they are in their sales cycle.

With CRM-based logic, we can:

- ✔ Trigger mailers at key sales stages
- ✔ Pause mail if the homeowner moves forward
- ✔ Customize messaging to include any variable data – name, projected monthly savings, etc.

And the best part? It's low-cost and fully automated. Each piece goes out the door personalized for $0.74 or less, with no manual coordination or team involvement required post-setup. So, if a homeowner received all 11 mailers in the current *Coulda, Shoulda* sequence (which many won't, since high-usage homes skip certain milestones or due to a homeowner being motivated by the mail to act and sign a contract), the total cost would still be only $8 per customer!

Now savvy solar business leaders, if you're spending hundreds to acquire one opportunity —why not spend $8 to keep them engaged? That's easy math, wouldn't you say? And we didn't stop at the *Coulda, Shoulda* Campaign. Now, we're triggering personalized mail at every stage of the funnel—from new lead nurture to contract signed, system upgrades, panel cleanings, and even post-install anniversaries. Each touchpoint reminds the customer how smart their decision was, celebrates their environmental impact, and nudges them to refer friends and earn rewards.

It's a full-lifecycle strategy—designed to sustain momentum, reduce fallout, and fuel organic growth through trust and retention. With a carefully thought-out strategy, we can stay top of mind with a homeowner for 18-24 months in a noninvasive manner, no clicks required.

While direct mail isn't the fastest source for lead generation, once someone's in the funnel, it becomes a conversion dynamo—amplifying engagement, building trust, and creating urgency.

I'm not going to dive deep into the behavioral science behind it yet (that's coming in Chapter 4), but here's the teaser: People don't buy based on logic—they buy based on feeling. And mail gives them something they can feel—i.e. the Solar Assault tagline - if you can touch it, you can trust it!

So, if you're still thinking of direct mail as a standalone campaign, think again. It is one part of the larger puzzle of your sales and marketing strategy. The future is full-funnel, personalized, and emotionally intelligent. That's the Solar Assault difference!

Other Mailable Marketing

Many dealers have found success beyond traditional direct mail by using RSVP mailing programs—high-end, targeted campaigns aimed at affluent homeowners. You've likely seen them: an invitation to a steak dinner or a glossy, personalized credit offer. These luxury card packs (also called RSVP Luxury Card Decks) feature premium offers from local businesses in home improvement, real estate, travel, and other upscale services. They're sent to qualified households with high income and home values, connecting brands with consumers who have serious buying power. For a broader reach, Valpak offers a similar shared mail advertising program but typically targets middle-income households with coupon-based local deals in a cost-effective, mass-distribution format.

Commercial Targeting: High-Impact FedEx Campaigns

When it comes to commercial solar, traditional direct mail is ineffective. Why? Because decision-makers rarely open their own mail, and gatekeepers like receptionists filter out anything that doesn't seem urgent.

One highly effective alternative is a targeted FedEx campaign—a strategy that dramatically increases the chances of your message landing directly in the hands of the right person. Unlike standard mail, FedEx packages are almost always opened by the intended recipient, making them a powerful tool for breaking through the noise.

CASE STUDY: EXIT PLANNING CAMPAIGN

My agency, Covert Communication, executed a similar campaign here in Hawaii for a financial services firm focused on exit planning, targeting construction company owners. Here's how the strategy worked:

1. Identified 20 high-potential business owners through research: name, address, years in business, size of company in revenue, etc.

2. Executed a three-step FedEx mailer sequence:

   - **Mailer #1:** A beautifully designed invitation to a "Lunch & Learn" on exit planning for their industry.

   - **Mailer #2:** A mini baseball bat with the tagline: *"When you're ready to break free."*

   - **Mailer #3:** A burner phone with a single number programmed, accompanied by the message: *"When you're ready to exit, there's only one call to make."*

The results? 50% of recipients called, leading to multiple high-value business sales.

Applying This to Commercial Solar

Using the same principles of creativity, industry lingo, and personalization, a FedEx campaign could be a game-changer for commercial solar. Here are a few ideas:

1. **Handcuffs with a note:** *"Tired of being a prisoner to the utility company?"*

2. **Luxury cigar & message:** *"When you're ready to smoke up the savings, give us a call."*

3. **LED lightbulb with custom engraving:** *"It's time to flip the switch on energy independence."*

The key? Be bold, be memorable, and make it impossible to ignore. This approach keeps costs low while maximizing ROI—making it one of the most effective strategies for engaging high-value commercial prospects.

We'll dive deeper into the behavioral science behind why this approach works, but for now, here's a preview of how combining reciprocity and scarcity can give your outreach real teeth with a unique mailer campaign.

The Play:

Send a personalized FedEx package informing the targeted business they've been hand-selected for an exclusive industry study. Emphasize that only five companies in their vertical and region are being offered this opportunity.

The Hook:

Make it simple and valuable:

- A comprehensive energy audit of their facility
- Only 12–24 months of utility bills required
- Drone footage of their site for evaluation (which they can keep and use for their own marketing)
- A full energy analysis report at no cost (a $2,500 value)

The Only Ask?

They allow their anonymized data to be used in a broader industry insights report.

No pressure. No risk. They feel valued, chosen, and curious. And they're motivated to act quickly—before the opportunity disappears.

The result? You've delivered real value, created a sense of exclusivity, and opened a natural path to a deeper solar conversation once the audit is revealed.

To Wrap Up Direct Mail

From EDDM campaigns and luxury card decks to personalized FedEx outreach and Solar Assault-style automation, one thing is clear: direct mail still delivers—when it's targeted, timely, and bold.

Data plays a crucial role in getting it right. There are many ways to acquire high-quality homeowner data, including services which offer detailed permit records (solar, roof, etc.) that can be filtered by issue date, pull date, expiration, or even bankrupt installer history—ideal for service and maintenance campaigns targeting orphaned systems.

While new homeowners may seem like attractive targets, they often aren't ready to buy. Without historical utility bills, they lack the context to understand potential savings, making early outreach premature. Unless you have a big budget and a long-term nurturing strategy, it's best to hold off for 12–18 months post them moving into the home before expecting meaningful conversions.

Another valuable insight: homeowners with children—regardless of age—are statistically more likely to adopt solar[5]. We attribute this to legacy thinking: the desire to pass down something meaningful, like energy independence and sustainability.

Whether you're engaging homeowners through shared mail or reaching commercial prospects with high-impact packages, the winning formula remains simple: make it valuable, make it memorable, and make it feel exclusive.

With the door now open, the next step is turning interest into action—through incentives, rebates, and promos that drive response rates not only from direct mail but across every touchpoint in your campaign.

Incentives, Rebates, and Promos

One of the most common—and effective—ways to increase solar leads is by offering a compelling incentive, rebate, or promotional offer. Whether driven by manufacturers or created at the company level, these programs are designed to create urgency and prompt immediate action.

A key detail to keep in mind with rebates is how they impact the customer's tax credit. To avoid reducing their eligible credit, the smart approach is to keep the full contract price intact and issue the rebate after installation—typically as a Visa gift card. This method allows customers to claim the full tax incentive while still receiving the benefit of a rebate.

My go-to vendor for managing these programs is Best Payment Solutions. They offer a streamlined platform that makes it incredibly easy to run:

---

5 https://www.sciencedirect.com/science/article/pii/S0301421522000933

- **Customer rebate programs**—automated post-install incentives

- **Referral rewards**—send gift cards instantly to customers or partners who refer business

- **Sales team contests and spiffs**—with real-time reporting and leaderboards

- **Review us rewards**—send gift cards to customers who upload screenshots of their reviews

It's quick to implement, simple to manage, and easy to track across campaigns—keeping everything clean for finance, operations, and sales. Best of all, it's cost-effective and makes it easy to show clear ROI. They handle all the 1099s and have experience working with the best — SunPower, Axia by Qcells, Powur, KIA, and many more.

Other common offers in the industry include:

- "We'll pay your power bill up to $1,200" as a way to ease the transition and create an immediate win. It's common that customers can pick how they leverage this offer—i.e., they could have the solar company start paying their bill at contract signing or opt to receive a check for the amount once the installation is complete.

- Free products like EV chargers, solar attic fans, or generators bundled with installation.

But one of the most unique and effective approaches I've seen comes from Evergreen Solar Solutions, a client based in Orlando, Florida, who's turned gifting into a dynamic customer experience and powerful closing tool.

CASE STUDY: THE SOLAR GETAWAY - HOW EVERGREEN MADE INCENTIVES IRRESISTIBLE

When I first connected with Evergreen Solar Solutions in 2023 through the SunPower network, I was instantly intrigued. While the company was still relatively new to solar—just two years in—the team behind it brought serious firepower: over 30 years of experience in the high-stakes world of timeshare sales.

Tony Milazzo, the founder, knew how to close. His background was built on high-volume, high-pressure, and high-reward selling—but what he wanted to do next was different. He saw an opportunity to take proven hospitality-style incentive strategies and bring them into solar, not as a gimmick, but as a way to build trust, spark excitement, and keep deals moving with momentum.

What happened next? Let's just say it involves family vacations, cruise ships, and a whole new way to win solar deals without dropping your price.

Tony believed that the timeshare model could work for solar. As he explained, "In timeshare, we had to sell fast, build value instantly, and overcome objections before they even came up. It was all about getting people emotionally invested in the idea of a reward before they even sat down. That's how timeshare wins—they get you hooked on the incentive. You're not just there for a pitch; you're there for the trip, the gift, the upgrade. And once someone imagines that reward, they're far more likely to stay open to the offer."

Now, solar isn't the same pitch but the principles carry over. People want to feel like they're getting something now, not just saving money over 25 years. The long-term ROI is great, but most homeowners are thinking in shorter cycles—bills, vacations and family budgets. So, we asked ourselves, *"How can we make it worth someone's time just to learn about solar?"* That's where the travel incentives came in.

We took what worked in the timeshare world—high-perceived-value rewards with low actual cost—and tailored it to solar, where trust and education are key. The result? A softer, more inviting entry point that doesn't feel like a sales trap. Just an invitation to learn and get rewarded for it.

Anna: So, what was the first incentive you rolled out?

Tony: Simple. "Take a meeting with us, and we'll give you a 3-day, 2-night mini vacation valued at $375." No strings, no gimmicks. Just a thank-you for your time. And if they sent over a utility bill before the consultation? We upgraded it to 4-days and 3-nights—valued at $575.

Anna: And how did people respond?

Tony: They loved it. It broke the ice, got people to engage, and they showed up. We made redemption easy—just a $100 refundable online credit card deposit to cover taxes and fees, which typically comes out to about $16 per night. And there's nothing shady about it—no hidden conditions, no timeshare presentations, just a clean, simple online booking process. Compared to companies still mailing checks or adding fine print? This felt like real value with zero hassle.

Anna: What about after the consultation? How did you use the incentive to help close the deal?

Tony: If the consultation went well—and most did—we'd say, "This feels like a great decision for your family. If you decide to move forward with Evergreen, we'll trade your mini vacation for a full trip to celebrate your smart choice."

The full vacation upgrade added a powerful emotional reward at the point of decision, which helped push people past the hesitation that usually creeps in when it's time to sign.

This approach was really designed to increase the close rate and minimize cancellations. The customer isn't just buying solar, they're picturing themselves on a cruise or a Vegas getaway, celebrating the fact that they made a smart financial move. That emotional anchor makes it harder to walk away.

And let's be honest, if your price is about the same as the guy down the street—and it usually is—this kind of offer makes it an easy decision. You're creating differentiation without lowering your price or squeezing margin. You're giving the customer a reason to say yes today.

Anna: Sounds like an unbeatable combo, a solar system and a vacation! What kind of trips are you offering that get people to say yes on the spot?

Tony: Our go-to offers are a Las Vegas getaway or a dream cruise—both with airfare included and valued over $2,000. But we've done it all: Hawaii, Disney, you name it. If the customer has a dream, we make it part of the pitch.

When people imagine themselves relaxing on a beach or making memories with their kids, going solar stops being just a financial choice, it becomes an easy win. We connect emotional payoff to a logical decision, and that's when the magic happens.

Anna: And for the skeptics out there—what's the catch? How do you make this affordable?

Tony: That's the beauty of it. The mini vacation—the marketing incentive—costs us about $10. The upgraded trip for customers who go solar cost us between $150 and $220 (or less with bulk purchases). We work with a travel partner that taps into unused hotel, airline, and cruise inventory and they know that with any type of promotions there is always a 'burn rate' meaning that some people never redeem their trip, which allows them to offer these amazing prices. So everyone wins, the dealer gets to pitch a high value incentive for the homeowner while keeping overall investment low, the travel partners win by having more people at their properties spending money. It's an overall economic booster compared with more traditional incentives we see dealers do i.e. a $500 Visa Gift Card.

Anna: What's been the overall impact?

Tony: Total game changer—more sits, higher close rates, fewer cancellations. Customers feel valued, and the team's excited to offer something memorable.

To Wrap Up Promos

Incentives, rebates, and promos remain some of the most effective tools in the solar marketer's playbook—when used strategically. Whether it's a manufacturer rebate, a utility bill buyout, a free product like an EV charger, or a travel-based incentive like Evergreen Solar Solutions' offers, the goal is the same: create urgency, increase perceived value, and guide the customer toward a confident yes.

As we've seen, the most effective offers are emotionally resonant, easy to redeem, and structured to protect the customer's tax credit eligibility (when applicable) while keeping your acquisition costs in check. These tools will become even more critical for dealers competing on similar equipment—especially as federal and state incentives fluctuate. With some tax credits now sunsetting or being paused, the ability to add meaningful value will become a key differentiator. And while these incentives may return in future legislative cycles, building a resilient sales strategy that doesn't rely solely on subsidies is essential for long-term growth.

Community Engagement through PR / Events

One of my favorite ways to generate leads is through what we call Breakout Public Relations (PR) initiatives—creative, attention-grabbing strategies that go beyond the typical playbook. These can be combined with traditional events to create bigger buzz and drive deeper engagement. We'll start by identifying quick-win event opportunities, explore how to host your own standout experiences, and wrap up with some of my favorite breakout PR ideas designed to spark creativity and attract high-value opportunities your way.

Events: Creating Memorable Moments that Generate Leads

Events shouldn't surprise anyone as they've long been a proven method for lead generation. Key opportunities include home & garden shows, home improvement expos, sustainability and green living fairs, local farmers markets, community fairs, new homeowner or first-time buyer seminars, builder and contractor trade shows, and of course chamber of commerce events or local business mixers.

Depending on your company's core audience—residential or commercial—it's a smart move to create a Marketing Activities Calendar (MAC) at the start of each fiscal year. This should outline known events as well as a wish list of those worth researching.

How Do You Decide Which Events to Attend?

You'll want to consider opportunity cost:

- What is the time commitment for your team?

- How many days is the event?

- What are the total costs for the booth, staffing, and branded materials?

- Will you stand out—or blend in?

If your booth isn't memorable, it's unlikely you'll generate the ROI you're hoping for. Ask for attendee estimates and vendor maps. Will you be near similar businesses? That's not necessarily a bad thing! I personally love being right next to competitors. It raises everyone's game and can lead to better-qualified prospects. It also creates a better experience for attendees, offering real choice and comparison.

Once you have that data, run the numbers. If 1,000 people are expected, and you use a 2% conversion rate, that's 20 potential qualified leads. Factor in how long the event lasts, the visibility of your booth, and your team's energy. Worth it? Maybe, it all depends on your sit and close rates.

Don't Just Show Up—Stand Out

Always have a fun and engaging event offer:

- Dress your team in LED light backpacks with mobile chargers, walking the floor and inviting people back to your booth for a speed charge or to win something cool.

- At outdoor events, set up solar-powered cooking stations— like a George Foreman Grill powered by a panel and battery (you can pretend) and then cook hot dogs for the first 100 people who opt in via text.

- Engage curiosity with a solar quiz using the "information gap" method to draw people in (more on that in Chapter 4).

Be bold. Be interactive. Make connections—and let the leads come to you.

⚠️ **ANNA'S TIP**

Always have offline backup methods to collect information. Not all venues have reliable internet. Bring business cards, offer physical collateral, and make sure your website is your mothership—everything should point back there for re-engagement after the event.

Create an Event

In addition to attending existing expos and fairs, one of the best ways to stand out is by creating your own events. These can range from post-installation celebrations, community-driven initiatives, and Lunch & Learns to fully online seminars—all of which can drive awareness, build trust, and generate leads.

Online Events

The pandemic normalized virtual learning, and many companies found success hosting online seminars on solar-related topics. These can include:

- Debunking solar myths
- How much solar do I need?
- Understanding NEM and local incentives
- HOA regulations and solar readiness

Tools like Eventbrite make it easy to manage RSVPs, while platforms like YouTube, RSS.com, and your own website help extend the reach of recorded sessions—driving long-term SEO value and building backlinks. Distributing content across multiple channels ensures you meet your audience where they are, whether they're browsing social media, checking email, or discovering content through search.

That said, leveraging exclusivity—like offering a seminar-only deal or keeping the session off public platforms—can drive urgency and boost live attendance. It's all about striking the right balance between access and allure.

In-Person: Lunch & Learns

You can also take a cue from financial advisors and host Lunch & Learn events by renting a meeting room and inviting local home or business owners. One creative example comes from our friends at Evergreen Solar, who adopted a page from the timeshare playbook—offering a 4-day, 3-night vacation valued at $575 in exchange for attending. The actual cost to the company? Just $20 per voucher (or less with bulk). High perceived value, low investment, big results.

Post-Sale Events: Interconnection "Flip the Switch" Parties

"Solarbrations" are a popular tactic—small block parties or gatherings held at the homeowner's property when their system was officially inter-connected. The salesperson would "flip the switch," neighbors would be invited via direct mail, and the event would include light snacks, fun give-aways, and a referral incentive tied to the host. These not only celebrated the install but also turned happy customers into evangelists.

> *"We used to offer the homeowner a $500 budget to host a solar social on their own timeline, they'd have a BBQ or party for neighbors and generate referrals. This made it less salesy, and the response was terrific!"*
>
> – Patrick Merrill, Solar Sales Leader since 2014

What is Breakout PR?

Breakout PR is all about bold, creative moments that demand attention. Unlike traditional PR—where you send out a generic press release that quickly becomes old news—breakout PR creates a newsworthy opportunity and pitches it directly to local media, making it more authentic and relevant. Start by assessing your brand's threshold for boldness. What's your comfort zone? And what's just outside it?

Let's be clear: I've done some wild stuff (yes, tattoo contests, guerilla sign kidnapping, and some I won't mention), but it's always legal, safe, and strategic. If you want to play it safer, you still have plenty of options. Here are a few of my personal favorites:

- Hilo Hattie Segway Fashion Show in Waikiki – I hired models and leveraged Segway of Hawaii to delight tourists.

- Mascot Bunny Airport Surprise – Mokulele Airlines "Island Jumping" for Easter, where we gave away hugs and eggs with prizes.

- "Toasty House" Gingerbread Contest – featuring community-made houses with Love's Bread to win 100,000 Hawaiian Miles.

See those and more examples at covertcommunication.com and be inspired by some of my brand heroes by checking out the "Breakout PR Inspirations" playlist on my YouTube channel.

How to Plan a Breakout PR Event

Start with imagination. Picture this: A homeowner's washing dishes, gazing out at the kids playing, someone's washing their car...It's a slice of the American dream. What would make that scene better?

Duh. Ice Cream.

Now imagine a bright blue, solar-branded ice cream truck rolling down the street,

playing *Here Comes the Sun.* People gather. Kids smile. And when that truck opens up—surprise—it's a mobile solar showroom! Storage systems, panels, EV chargers, the works. You hand out free popsicles (Costco-style—no food permit needed). Add a donation option to a local school or church, and now you've layered community goodwill onto the stunt.

More Community-Driven Ideas

If ice cream trucks aren't your thing, consider:

- Donating solar-powered trash cans with your logo to a high-traffic public area.

- Donate a playhouse for a community park, painting the rooftop with solar panels (or use stickers). Place your logo on the door or inside the house to get some well-deserved branding on your good deed.

- Sponsoring a community garden (complete with seed packet direct mailer invitations: *"Come plant the future with us— Saturday at 3pm!"*)

No budget? No problem. These cost next to nothing but sweat equity:

Street Team Activations

- **Solar Cheerleaders** "GOOOO SOLAR!" hyping up sustainability at intersections or events.

- **Solar Superheroes** performing random acts of kindness in logo gear: feed parking meters, hand out dollar bills, carry groceries, pick up trash—record it all and post on social.

- **Charging Station Booth** at farmers markets: "15 minutes to charge, 15 minutes to learn about solar."

Breakout PR doesn't just get attention—it builds brand love, local loyalty, and often, media coverage worth tens of thousands. The key is this: think different, stay ethical, and commit fully.

And the best part? You don't need a full production crew. All you need is a standard camera to record your event. Capture long, continuous segments (limit the cutting), and think like a news producer—if the story aired on TV, what would the anchor say over your footage? I like to use 10–20 second clips and submit 1–2 minutes of total footage, stripped of sound. Upload a high-res, professional version to Vimeo, then create a smaller, easily shareable version for newsrooms. Make it simple, make it fun—and make it look like it belongs on the morning news (more warm and fuzzy than evening news but hey go for both, just remember that the news crews typically change midday so you'll need to call again if you didn't make the cut to reintroduce your concept!)

Ready to create your own spectacle? Start brainstorming. For those not very creative, hire one!

Next up, let's keep the momentum going by diving deeper into inspired programs that combine community engagement with referral building.

Community Fundraisers

A creative twist on traditional fundraising: instead of selling cookies or raffle tickets, schools, sports teams, and local nonprofits can raise money by helping connect homeowners with solar consultants. It's a win-win—supporters generate funds for their cause while promoting clean energy in the community. A typical arrangement might be:

- $100 raised for every completed demo conducted with homeowner
- $500 if a deal closes

It's a high-reward, low-effort model that can generate serious funding for the organization—and valuable leads for your team. It's like building your own team of door knockers, but with built-in community trust and purpose-driven motivation behind every interaction. No, it's not child labor. It's Girl Scout cookies on steroids.

The possibilities are endless. Ask yourself: how can we create memorable, high-value moments in our community? From there, it's all about leveraging partnerships and having the right systems in place to manage the flow of leads and referrals.

Next, let's explore how to take that momentum even further by leveraging vertical partnerships to generate referrals that truly resonate.

Vertical Partnerships

Vertical partnerships involve teaming up with companies that already serve homeowners or business owners. Common examples include roofers, HVAC contractors, landscapers, architects, builders, developers, real estate agents, car dealerships, financial advisors, retailers, and even HR departments. For example, companies like Disney, AT&T, and many more offer additional benefits for employees, which have included in the past discounts to go solar as part of the former SunPower affiliate program.

There are endless opportunities but the key to success lies in creating true value that leads to steady, long-term referral flows. Let's start with a foundational truth: People don't like change. But they do want more money and more freedom—if it's easy and feels like a natural value add.

This means that when setting up referral partnerships, you need to think about how the offer trickles down inside the partner's organization. If it's confusing, intrusive, or out of step with their workflow, it won't last.

A Smart Example: EV Car Dealerships

Say you want to partner with a car dealership that sells electric vehicles. Great fit, right? EVs need home charging, and solar is the perfect match. But here's what not to do: Don't try to get the car salesperson to add solar into the car pitch. That's clunky and kills the sale.

Instead, think strategically. The ideal moment is when the deal is being finalized—often by a finance manager or service advisor whose job is to present add-ons like maintenance packages, tire warranties, and coatings.

That person is already in the value-add mindset. Train them to say something like, "Do you already have solar at home or need a Level 2 charger installed? We work with a trusted local partner. If you'd like, I can share your contact info so they can provide a complimentary home assessment. Mention my name for a special discount."

Boom. Easy, seamless, and high-converting.

Becoming the Solar Arm of Another Business

Another approach is to integrate directly into a partner's offering as their solar division. In the Powur network, this is known as an Enterprise Account. They have designed their platform to facilitate lead sharing, role splitting, and transparent commissions.

Let's say Pops HVAC has no interest in selling solar. That's fine—they can stay focused on what they do best while allowing your solar team to introduce themselves to customers as *"Pops HVAC's new solar division."*

You manage everything: outreach, quoting, and contracts. The customer stays in Pops' portal (so Pops still gets attribution), and the revenue is shared—say, 70/30 in favor of the solar sales team. That often feels (and is!) more generous than a one-time flat referral fee. And the costs? A nominal $350 per month for the platform, which quickly pays for itself and makes the process easy to manage and transparent for all parties. Note: Powur has recently, as of Q2-2025, rolled out some new pricing models and new ways to build teams for less. Join my team at annacovert.com; we'd love to support you!

Real Estate Agents = Dual Commission Opportunity

Realtors are an especially powerful partner because they're already helping clients buy or sell homes—and many of those homes have existing solar systems or solar potential. By working with a knowledgeable solar partner, the agent can:

- Determine the value of existing systems
- Navigate lease transfers or system ownership questions
- Refer clients looking to add solar through green mortgages or HELOCs

This builds the realtor's value and expands your reach. Solar companies should host workshops or webinars to make realtors feel confident discussing solar. Provide FAQs and quick sheets they can share with buyers and sellers alike.

A Smart Example: Retail Venues Like Costco & Home Depot

Having a branded booth inside a big-box store like Costco or Home Depot can generate solid leads—but it also comes with high costs, logistical headaches, and strict store policies. You're paying for floor space, staffing, and visibility but not always getting consistent ROI.

Now here's the twist: What if you could get the same value without the physical booth?

I haven't seen anyone pull this off yet—but imagine creating a referral network within the store itself, no setup required. The key? Build relationships with department staff who already interact with customers making solar-adjacent purchases—like HVAC systems, water heaters, or energy-efficient appliances.

Say a customer is upgrading to a high-efficiency washer and dryer. That associate could say:

"A lot of customers who switch to energy-efficient appliances also look into solar to save even more on their utility bills. If you're curious, we work with a trusted local solar installer who offers free home estimates. Want me to have someone reach out?"

No hard sell. No booth. Just smart, contextual referrals at the right time.

This kind of setup might be tricky in large national chains. Think local.

Independent hardware stores, garden centers, pool supply shops, boutique home goods retailers—and even local roofers—are often open to behind-the-scenes partnerships. A simple referral bonus, QR code, or co-branded card can turn them into quiet but powerful allies supporting your growth in the community. No matter how great the partnership concept, if you can't back it up with:

- Transparent reporting
- Fast, reliable commission payouts
- A smooth follow-up process
- Ready-to-use collateral they can easily share
- A dedicated contact they can reach with questions

...the relationship won't last. Partnerships thrive on trust and simplicity.

Up next: How to leverage technology to automate partner tracking, follow-ups, and referrals—so nothing falls through the cracks.

The Art of Referrals

By now, it shouldn't be a surprise that in solar, referrals are essential. They can make or break a company. While marketing campaigns can spark interest and drive leads, it's word-of-mouth that truly builds trust, especially in an industry where the stakes—and the price tags—are high. People trust their neighbors, family, and coworkers more than any ad, and the businesses that lead the pack are the ones that harness this truth. The most successful companies are the ones that prioritize customer experience and back it up with a well-oiled referral process that's easy, rewarding, and consistent.

> *"It all comes down to discipline—especially when it comes to customer acquisition costs. When we shut off paid leads and focused on referrals, our CAC dropped from $2,000 to around $500–$600 per job. We had a brief dip in volume, but the payoff was worth it. Hitting a 98% referral rate wasn't easy, but it was the clearest sign we were building something sustainable. If people trust you enough to refer you to their neighbors or business partners, that's the gold standard."*
>
> – Paul Sullivan, Solar Industry Leader since 2006

This principle holds true across the board—whether you're installing rooftop systems for homeowners, managing multi-site commercial projects, or brokering utility-scale land deals. Referrals are the thread that ties it all together.

As the solar coaster continues to shift, I've seen several dealers pivot out of residential and into commercial and utility-scale opportunities. But no matter the vertical, growth still hinges on relationships and trust—on someone vouching for you and saying, *"This is the team you want."* In large-scale and commercial solar, that trust often comes through repeated visibility. When stakeholders consistently see your trucks, crews, or equipment on-site, confidence builds before you ever pick up the phone.

Later in this book, you'll hear directly from solar veterans who successfully transitioned out of residential by relying almost entirely on referral networks—with impressive results. That said, there's still enormous potential for residential-only companies to thrive on referrals alone.

The real question is scale: how big do you want to grow, and how many mouths do you need to feed on your sales team?

For a company closing 30 deals a month, a 100% referral-based model is possible—if you've done the work, built trust, and have a strong local presence. One of my California-based dealers, Ambrose Solar, is a perfect example. Their brand promise— *"We're with you from installation to optimization—and every service call in between"*—has earned them deep customer loyalty. From service and maintenance to upgrades and replacements, they stay with the homeowner every step of the way.

Because of that commitment, they've weathered the ups and downs of the solar coaster with a referral network that continues to deliver year after year. Today, we also run full-funnel digital campaigns and direct mail to help scale their growth—but those efforts are far more effective thanks to the foundation of trust already built through referrals.

The Technology to Support Referrals

Most referral programs are structured in tiers. There's usually a small initial payout when the referral results in a consultation or sits for a demo—typically between $50 and $100. If the project moves forward, a second, larger payment is issued upon installation, ranging from $250 to $1,500 or more. These payouts can vary depending on what's included in the final system—solar PV (alone), batteries, EV chargers, or pool heating all can come with different referral values. The more value added, the more rewarding it is for both the customer and the referrer.

> ⚠️ **ANNA'S TIP**
>
> Pay attention to the process. A great referral program is simple to use, easy to track, and delivers fast, transparent rewards. Without those things in place, even the most loyal customers can lose motivation to refer.

To manage referrals, popular tools include Get The Referral (GTR), Snoball.com, and Best Payment Solutions. There's also the old-school approach—submitting referrals via a form and entering them manually into the CRM or using tools like webhooks, APIs, or Zapier for automated lead ingestion. But manual processes often lead to human error, missed payouts, and hurt feelings—one of the fastest ways to lose trust and future business when someone doesn't receive their promised reward.

Just as critical is communication. Referrals dry up fast if advocates (the people referring) are left in the dark. Solar deals take time—weeks or even months (dare I say years?) to close and install. If your advocate doesn't hear anything back, they'll stop asking and, eventually, stop referring. They deserve updates. Was the lead contacted? Did they sign? Are they moving forward? Without that feedback loop, your program loses momentum quickly.

You'll also need to manage 1099s for any individual earning $600 or more in a calendar year—a logistical headache. That's why most larger companies eventually partner with a platform to streamline payments, track referral status, and provide clear reporting by salesperson, product type, and bonus structure. It removes the friction and keeps everyone—advocates, reps, and finance—on the same page.

Here's a breakdown of the most common tools my clients use:

Get The Referral (GTR)

GTR is an app available on iOS and Android. Customers use a unique code, and the app rebrands itself with your company's logo. It replaced an earlier, clunkier version that required Apple Developer credentials and was a nightmare to manage.

The app includes robust backend tracking—up to nine customizable project milestones—and allows both advocates and sales teams to follow progress. But the tech does require setup, and if customers don't download the app, communication can fall apart. When I sold solar for Sunspear Energy, I'd ask customers to download it during the sales visit:

"Hey <homeowner>, we're running a promo right now—you can be your own first referral."

Even if they didn't buy that day, I now had a touchpoint via push notifications. Some dealers went further—if the customer didn't download the app, the rep didn't get paid. That drove 100% compliance. But despite the strong initial push, many agency accounts I helped onboard eventually canceled due to inactivity.

The key is leadership and process. Dealers who saw long-term success had executive buy-in and structured systems in place to keep the app and referral program visible. That included automated follow-ups, seasonal campaigns, and internal contests to keep reps engaged. It's not a "set it and forget it" tool. Like any part of your sales funnel, it needs to be actively promoted and maintained to drive results.

Snoball

Snoball launched in 2023 following a strategic split from BestCompany. com, which was later acquired by Modernize in 2024. While still loosely affiliated, Snoball has carved out its own lane by taking a more hands-on, streamlined approach to customer referrals. Using real people and AI-assisted workflows, Snoball texts your customers directly—no app needed. Customers simply reply with a name and number, and the platform feeds it into your CRM. From there, referral payouts are automatically triggered based on bi-directional mapped milestones like demo ran, contract signing, or installation complete.

We've piloted Snoball with two clients so far and seen excellent results 2-3% referral rates from outreach to legacy customers, but the pricing model is best suited for companies doing 30+ sales per month with a solid customer base to tap into. An added bonus: their outreach scripting often generates excellent Google reviews—which are worth their weight in gold.

Best Payment Solutions (BPS)

Best Payment Solutions is much more than a payment processor—it's a full-service growth engine. At the heart of their platform is the Triple R approach: Referrals, Rebates, and Reviews. While they do a great job at a lot of things, one of the biggest pain points for my agency/clients has always been verifying customer reviews. With so many platforms and user-names that rarely match customer records, it's a time-consuming night-mare to confirm who left a review so we can issue a thank-you gift card.

After being introduced to BPS and beginning our consulting work together, I brought up this major pain point—and I was blown away by how quickly and effectively they solved it. Best Payment Solutions rolled out a feature that handled it beautifully. Now, customers just enter their name, select the review platform, and upload a screenshot. From there, the system automatically verifies (with client approval) the review and sends the gift card—no chasing, no confusion. The result? More reviews (happier customers), less admin, and faster trackable and reportable rewards.

And the best part? The full Triple R platform is just $599 per year plus a nominal gift card transaction fee, making it one of the most cost-effective marketing and payment solutions on the market today, and the full campaign setup (for most) happens in under 14 days.

Powur Network

As mentioned earlier, this platform offers flexible commission-splitting options for teams in nearly every configuration imaginable. It also includes the Ambassador app, which allows solar companies to manage referral payouts to homeowners. The $1,000 referral reward is automatically deducted from the total commission and paid directly to the home-owner—streamlining the entire process.

However, this setup only works for systems that are both designed and sold through Powur. For companies operating outside the Powur ecosys-tem, this functionality isn't available. To put it in context: the referral must result in a Powur system sale in order for the payout to be managed through the app—you can not sell a different product and still use the platform to process the referral.

To Wrap Up Technology

Technology can make things easier, faster, and more scalable—but it's not a substitute for execution. Success still comes down to people. You need a team that communicates well, follows through, and keeps the customer experience front and center.

The right platform lays the foundation, but it's your process and consistency that drive results. I've seen plenty of referral and rebate programs with strong tools behind them, but without clear ownership, they fizzle out. If you make an offer, honor it. Every broken promise chips away at your brand.

Next up, we'll conclude the organic leads chapter with one of the most popular and controversial strategies: Door-Knocking.

Door-Knocking - Because Not Everyone Googles "Solar Savings"

Like it or not, door-knocking is still one of the most effective ways to generate solar leads—and no one does it better than Michael O'Donnell, aka MOD. He's not just a top performer; he's the *top* rooftop solar sales-person in the world, with multiple Double Golden Door Awards and a sales record that speaks volumes.

With over 25 years of experience in sales and senior sales leadership, Mike brings unmatched expertise to the table. As Partner and Vice President of Sales at SunSolar Solutions—Arizona's largest solar sales and installation company with over $80 million in annual revenue—he continues to set the pace for the industry.

Since releasing his book, Mike has only doubled down. He's still breaking records, mentoring rising talent, and showing up as a go-to keynote speaker and podcast guest across the solar space.

If you're serious about mastering door-to-door solar leads that produce sales, I highly recommend his book *No Matter Watt!: The Recipe to a 7-Figure Income in Sales.* His strategies are high-impact and have proven effective nationwide—even though some companies still view door-knocking as aggressive or outdated. Like any sales method, success comes down to how it's done. When approached with professionalism and purpose, it works—and Mike is living proof.

As Mike often says, "Even a poor knocker can book 3 appointments from 100 knocks a day. With a 30% close rate, that's 1 sale—or roughly a $3,500 to $7,000 commission. A good knocker can book 7 out of 100 and close 3 to 4."

The formula is simple: it's math. And when done consistently, it delivers.

Door-knocking becomes even more effective in teams, especially during a blitz—multiple reps canvassing the same neighborhood together. It boosts morale, increases coverage, and enhances safety. I recommend tools like Spotio, RepCard, or SalesRabbit to boost speed-to-lead, track rep activity, and keep your team aligned and accountable.

Just like the traditional setter-closer model, door knockers can work in separate roles, or take the full-cycle approach by setting and closing their own deals. This not only increases trust with the homeowner but often improves close rates.

All of this brings us to a crucial shift in mindset. There are two primary philosophies in solar sales: hard selling and soft selling. I've worked with clients on both sides, and there's no one-size-fits-all method. It comes down to your company's values and how you bring them to life through your culture and customer experience.

While I highly recommend picking up a copy of Mike's book, I also had the chance to sit down with him to hear how the industry has evolved since its release in January 2023—and what trends he's seeing now out in the field.

Anna: How has door knocking evolved in the solar industry? Is it still effective?

Mike: Absolutely—100%. Even with all the digital strategies out there, door knocking is still the most cost-effective and reliable way to introduce someone to solar. No overhead, no ad spend—just effort. You're showing up with knowledge and a willingness to connect. If you're good, you can turn nothing into something.

I use an Indeed service to meet about 15 job-seekers a week and walk them through the numbers: knock on 100 doors, have 30 conversations, and usually get 1–3 real opportunities. That math hasn't changed in years—it's like gravity in this business.

Digital leads can work, but many ghost. At the door, you've got their full attention. You're taking someone from *"not even thinking about solar"* to *"maybe I should consider it."* That shift is the most valuable part of the sale—and door knocking still does it best.

Anna: That seems like a grind. How do you stay motivated through the rejections?

Mike: Rejection is part of the game—you have to expect it, embrace it, and push through. You might get 30 straight "no's," but if you keep going, you'll find the three who say, *"Tell me more,"* and one will likely become a customer. That one "yes" could be worth $5,000 to $10,000.

Mindset is everything. I tell new reps: every "no" is paying you—you just haven't seen the deposit yet. Think of it like moving $100 from one pocket to the other with each rejection. You're getting paid to keep going. The hardest part isn't knocking—it's managing your emotions. Most rejections aren't personal; they're about timing, stress, or someone's mood. Once you stop taking it personally, you start seeing every "no" as a step toward a "yes." That's the real path to six- and seven-figure success in solar.

Anna: The industry's evolved a lot in recent years. How would you describe the landscape today?

Mike: In one word? Shifted. The gold rush is over. From 2015 to 2020, solar was booming— low interest rates, big incentives, and easy bill-swap pitches made closing simple. That era's gone.

Now, with higher interest rates and cautious consumers, that same $180 solar payment doesn't feel like a win when it matches—or exceeds—the utility bill. People are scrutinizing every dollar, and sales have dropped across the board. Big names like Sunrun, Sunnova and SunPower have taken hits.

Why? Too many reps were trained to sell hype, not value. Some over-promised or misled customers, and now the industry is feeling the fallout. The good news? There's still massive opportunity—but only for those who lead with integrity, math, and transparency. If you can educate and build trust, you'll thrive. If not, you won't last.

Anna: What's your take on transparency in solar sales?

Mike: It's everything. Transparency isn't optional—it's the foundation of trust. Too many reps still mislead customers, like promising 100% offset without explaining fees or seasonal shifts or saying they'll "get a check" for the tax credit when that's not how it works. That's not just misleading—it's fraud.

These tactics fuel distrust, cancellations, and lawsuits. Even honest reps must work twice as hard to earn back credibility.

At SunSolar, we train reps to educate, not manipulate. We walk customers through the real math—offset, net metering, long-term savings—and never gloss over the details. Solar doesn't need hype to sell. When presented honestly, it stands on its own.

One major red flag? Reps are removing the tax credit from monthly payments to show a lower number. If the customer doesn't qualify or apply it, their payment jumps—and they weren't warned. That's bait and switch. The best sale is when a customer trusts you enough to refer their friends. That only happens when you lead with integrity.

Anna: Why do you believe that closing in the first meeting is so important in solar sales?

Mike: Because that first meeting is your best—and often only—real window of opportunity. When someone agrees to sit down with you, they're in an open, decision-making mindset. They're listening, evaluating, and seriously considering a change. That moment of clarity is rare, and if you don't help them take action right then, odds are they never will. The iron cools fast.

Our job isn't to pressure people—it's to help them help themselves. We're not selling snake oil. The math is clear. The savings are real. The value is there. But people are human. If they don't sign, they go back to life—distractions, doubts, Google rabbit holes, and opinions from people who don't have the full picture. And fear sets in: fear of commitment, fear of making a mistake. Even when the deal makes perfect sense, that hesitation kills momentum.

But if they do sign? Now they're committed. They have time to call their accountant, run the numbers again, and do their due diligence—and they will, because now they have a reason to. Commitment activates clarity. It's about guiding them through the fog of indecision and helping them take a step toward something better. If you wait, they won't. If they move forward, they win.

Anna: What's your strategy to get the homeowner to sign that day?
Mike: I make it clear this is their one shot with me. I tell them, "My job is to share this with as many people as possible—I'm not coming back." It's not a tactic; it's the truth. I'm not in the business of chasing leads. If they want to wait, they can call the office later, but it won't be me showing up. What I'm offering isn't just a solar quote—it's a moment of momentum. If they sign today, they get my number, my support, and someone who knows their situation. If they wait, that personal connection is gone.

I'm not here to pressure anyone—I'm here to bring clarity. The numbers already make sense. My role is to help them take action while the opportunity is right in front of them. Because let's be honest—most people who say "I'll think about it" never actually do.

Anna: How is SunSolar handling the rising cancellation rates and declining sit rates affecting the industry?
Mike: It's a real challenge across the industry—even with door knocking, sit rates have dropped from 70% to 30–40%, and cancellations are way up. A big factor is permit poaching—competitors pull public data and try to undercut deals, creating doubt.

At SunSolar, we fight that with clarity from the start. We walk customers through the real math, set honest expectations, and make sure they understand every step. That's why our sit rates are higher, and cancellations are lower—we focus on informed decisions, not pressure. When the value is clear, people stay.

Anna: Any final thoughts for someone thinking about getting into door-to-door solar sales?

Mike: If you're thinking about stepping into door-to-door solar sales, here's what you need to understand: this job isn't about convincing people that solar is good. Solar *is* good. The savings are real. The product is powerful. The value proposition is solid. What you're really doing is helping someone take action today—because that's the hard part. It's not the information; it's the decision.

When you knock on someone's door, you're catching them off guard. They weren't planning to talk about energy bills or tax credits—they were probably just doing the dishes. Your job is to guide them through that moment of interruption, help them see the opportunity, and give them a reason to say "yes" now instead of later. Because here's the truth: if they wait, they lose the rep, they lose the offer, and they lose momentum. And you don't get a second chance to create urgency. That's why we train our reps to find the *Golden Easter Egg*—that one person out of a hundred who's not just polite or curious, but ready. And you don't find them by luck—you find them by knocking. Consistently. Professionally. Skillfully. The opportunity is out there, but you have to do the work to uncover it.

I like to explain it like this: imagine you go to a dance, and your job is to ask 30 people to dance. Twenty-seven of them say no—maybe even rudely. Most people would quit right there. They'd say, "I'm not a dancer," and sit down for the rest of the night. But what if you pushed through those no's? What if three people said yes—and one of them turned out to be the best partner in the room? That's sales. It's not about rejection. It's about persistence. It's about understanding that the "no" is just the hallway to the "yes."

And once you realize that—once you detach from the rejection and focus on the process—you'll unlock a career that can change your life. We've seen people go from unemployed to making six figures within a year. But it starts with showing up, asking to dance, and being ready when some-one says yes.

To Conclude this Section

While door knocking remains one of the highest-ROI strategies in solar, it doesn't come without scrutiny. Reports of scammers impersonating utility reps have led to real safety concerns—particularly in states like Florida—and some HOAs have responded by restricting or banning door-to-door sales altogether.

That's why it's critical your team follows all local regulations, carries proper identification, and uses smart tactics like leaving door hangers to create a touchpoint even when no one answers. In HOA-restricted areas, another effective approach is to engage during active installations—intro-ducing yourself to neighbors, offering a card, answering questions, and turning curiosity into trust. These proactive, respectful touches can lead to highly qualified leads.

When done right—with smart targeting, digital tracking, and ethical execution—door knocking still delivers. Pair it with targeted direct mail to reinforce brand recognition, and you have one of the most effective outreach combinations in the business.

That said, not all door-to-door campaigns are created equal. Rising cancellation and no-show rates are often rooted in shady sales tactics—misleading proposals, permit poaching, and rushed contracts. That's why I sat down with Mike to dig into what's really happening in the field. Closing on the first meeting requires more than numbers; it demands trust, timing, and disciplined execution.

But not everyone agrees. In Chapter 3, we'll hear from another client who takes a very different stance. Their company doesn't allow same-day signings at all—yet they've built a thriving business by leading with long-form consultations and a relationship-first sales model. We'll explore how this soft-sell approach contrasts with hard-sell strategies and what it takes to make it work.

Then in Chapter 4, we'll look at companies embracing a hybrid approach—combining the urgency of direct sales with the trust-building of consultative selling. Because the real magic often happens somewhere in between.

Now that we've explored the many ways to generate a steady flow of self-generated leads, it's time to dive into paid leads.

CHAPTER 2:

PAID LEAD PROGRAMS

Not a day goes by without a client asking if I've heard of the latest "ABC" lead company. New providers are popping up constantly, making big promises, many of them empty. While lead programs remain the backbone for many solar companies, lead quality is heavily influenced by seasonality, regulatory shifts, market competition, and the growing threat of digital media fraud. These variables change fast and often without warning.

Too often, solar companies blame lead providers for poor results while neglecting basic best practices in outreach, follow-up, and performance tracking. And because the landscape changes quickly—new players emerge, policies shift, and results vary—I'm not calling out specific providers here. My priority is fairness, and the reality is, things move fast. Instead, my goal is to equip you with the right questions and criteria so you can spot red flags early and align with trusted, high-performing partners.

The reality is clear: those who fail to adapt will struggle. But those who take the time to evolve—meeting customers where they are, using smarter tools, better messaging, and more human experiences–will thrive in this next era of solar.

When it comes to buying leads, most programs fall into two distinct camps—marketing companies and manufacturers. Each comes with its own pros, cons, and traps to watch out for. But it goes deeper than just who's selling you the leads—it's about where those opportunities are originating from. Whether you're buying through a provider, a network, or a trusted manufacturer, the true source of the traffic—how it was generated, who it was targeting, and what expectations were set–will impact your results.

So, to kick things off, let's break down the different types of paid lead programs and the most common pitfalls to avoid.

Types of Paid Lead Programs

1. Flat Price per Appointment

- Dealers pay a set price per appointment ($250-$500).

- Programs allow for refunds or replacement appointments in some cases including out-of-territory leads, or mobile/ manufactured homes.

- Partner Considerations:

  o How are appointments confirmed? Is there a handoff process from the lead provider?

  o Are they booking in-person, virtually, or both?

  o What communication is sent to the customer? Overloading them can reduce trust. This also includes what brand name they're using to generate leads (i.e., website URLs, vanity names like "Energy For America"), which is important to ask as many leads quickly become poor due to the solar company thinking the customer opted in from ABC Solar, but in fact they were on a website for CDE Solar and now don't remember agreeing to meet.

2. Price per Demo Run

- Dealers only pay if the demo is completed. Pricing varies by call center or setter agreement in place.

- Works best when there's strong tracking and trust between sales teams and lead providers.

3. Price per Watt Sold

- Lead providers earn a commission per watt sold (e.g., $0.20 per watt).

- Challenges:

  o Sales conversion rates from sit to sale vary dramatically (10%-75%), making it hard to predict commissions.

  o Less control over the sales process. This should only be considered if you have an established track record with that solar company and sales team. Closely monitor lead sources responsible for generating the sales so you don't work with a partner who is not properly qualifying appointments, which wastes valuable time of your sales team.

4. Price per Lead *(Most Common!)*

- Dealers pay per lead, making quality control and speed-to-lead critical.

- Lead-to-appointment rates range from 5% to 30% (If they promise more, walk away slowly or make them prove it—not testimonials but actual hard facts or a test campaign that is 100% refundable).

- Billing structures:

  o **Flat rate** (e.g., $15-$250+ per fresh lead)

    ■ **Aged Data:** These can also be purchased as bulk data from providers based on criteria such as permits pulled, homeowners who were previously interested in solar, new or recently moved homeowners, etc. The price varies by market and age of the data (7-30 days, 30-60 days, 60-90 days, 90-180 days, 6-12 months, 12 months plus).

o **Variable pricing** (e.g., auction-based)

⚠ ANNA'S TIP

Rather than bidding by state or county, if you take the time to build campaigns with zip code buckets – good, better, best– then you can often find some big wins in places that have fewer solar companies competing for the same leads, which drive up the auction price. Some companies, like CEE (clean energy executives), do provide insights in their grow tab to help identify opportunity but I have personally never seen a recommendation go down in bid price, only up. So, you must play the game yourself and be proactive. No matter what platform, always reach out to our rep and ask specific questions on bid adjustments by zip code; they're eager to help you win.

---

o **Lead Tiers** (affects pricing and exclusivity):

■ **Premium Leads (Tier 1) / Exclusive Leads**: More qualified (they say); should be sold to fewer dealers. Exclusive leads are only supposed to be sold to one dealer, but...the jury is still out!

■ **Standard Lead (Tier 2 or 3) / Non-Exclusive Leads**: Sold to 2-4 dealers based on competition.

■ **Blended Leads**: Some platforms force dealers to accept a mix of lead types without clear distinction. Personally, I don't trust those. After multiple reviews, I couldn't find any consistent evidence that the top-tier leads were more qualified than the lower-cost ones. But hey—that's just *Anna-lytics*. Proceed accordingly.

■ **Warm Transfers**: Live customer handoff vs. standard lead transfers. These are phone calls. A warm transfer means the lead provider remains on with the homeowner, and then, once the solar company answers, they introduce the homeowner before dropping off the call.

Common Lead Program Challenges & Best Practices

1. Lead Quality Issues

Many dealers report that their company profile settings are not properly considered when third parties sell them a lead. Common challenges include:

- Homeowners who already have solar.

- Leads for mobile or manufactured homes (which may not qualify).

- Leads outside the correct utility or coverage area.

- Customers are misled by ads, believing solar is free.

- Not the homeowner or say they never agreed or opted into a lead funnel.

- Bad contact info—email, phone, or address (not verified).

⚠ **ANNA'S TIP**

Always request examples of the ads used by your lead provider. Are they driving traffic to a landing page they control, or just reselling third-party publisher leads? If they refuse to share those details, walk away. I cut ties with a popular lead source for this exact reason—too many reports of shady YouTube ads promising "free solar" and zero transparency. You're building a brand—don't settle for sloppy leads. Swipe left and stay classy.

What's Their Return Policy? (And Why You'd Better Ask)

Return policies vary by provider and lead type, but here's the truth: you need to read both the fine print *and* between the lines. Some platforms (not naming names) technically allow returns—but if you exceed a 10% return rate, they'll drop you. That kind of double standard drives me crazy. Either you stand behind your leads or you don't.

To protect your investment:

- Set up a clear CRM process to track and submit returns within the allowed window.

- Watch for red flags: If a provider won't let you choose lead types or integrate campaign data into your CRM, walk away. Your lead source should fit your system—not the other way around.

- Clarify make-goods: If leads fall outside your agreed-upon filters, they should be replaced. No excuses. If they refuse, that's a deal-breaker.

Transparency, control, and accountability are not optional. These are essential pillars for protecting your ad spend and maximizing ROI.

Common Valid Lead Return Reasons (within seven days):

- Outside your selected geographies
- Phone number is disconnected
- Duplicate lead (previously sent by provider)
- Job-seeker
- Another contractor
- Not a homeowner
- Already has PV installed
- Provider test leads
- Duplex or condominium
- Mobile/Manufactured homes

Common Unacceptable Return Reasons:

- Electric bill amount (too low)
- Utility company restrictions
- Homeowner not interested
- Homeowner is retired (fixed income or low usage)
- Homeowner did not pass credit check
- Not enough savings shown
- Roof in poor condition
- Too much shading for viable production
- Aesthetic concerns or HOA limitations

By staying proactive and ensuring your team properly logs and processes returns, you can minimize wasted spend and hold lead providers accountable for quality. No joke—I've personally witnessed *well* over

$30,000 in losses in a single year from companies that didn't have a clear process in place.

And no, most lead providers do not offer bi-directional CRM integration, so you need the process buttoned up. Your team must understand the implications of missing return windows or failing to tag bad leads, and there should be real consequences if they drop the ball. They need to be in this with you. Every lost return is lost revenue, and it adds up fast. Making lead return compliance part of your team's performance reviews is mission critical. And remind them: bad leads don't just cost the company money—they zap your reps' time, energy, and motivation.

Without a proper feedback loop, bad leads keep coming, and providers keep getting paid. If returns are not submitted quickly, the data loses value. It becomes harder to validate, harder to dispute, and less likely to trigger any course correction. Timely reporting is the only way to protect your pipeline and ensure your marketing dollars are working for you.

Here is the good news: high-quality lead providers welcome feedback. They rely on it to identify underperforming publishers, shut down bad campaigns, and reallocate budgets toward campaigns that deliver. By reporting issues early and clearly, you are helping to optimize the entire program. Light the way, solar Jedi!

2. Scheduling and Availability Issues

Appointment providers often:

- Ignore dealer availability, scheduling last-minute meetings with no prep time to generate proposals.

- Book in-person appointments in far-off locations without considering coverage.

- For lead purchases, this includes ingesting leads too early or on days without in-office coverage to confirm appointments or route them properly. For example, if a lead comes in on Saturday at 6 p.m. for a Monday appointment, but no one's working Sunday, that lead is already cold by the time your team makes contact. Timing matters and delayed follow-up kills momentum.

> ⚠️ **ANNA'S TIP**
>
> Don't let bad timing sink your sales. Your provider should integrate leads or appointments on a controlled schedule so you can manage volume by day, time, and team capacity. If you run virtual appointments, ask if they support round-robin calendars—this ensures leads are auto-assigned based on availability and boosts speed-to-lead.

For example, we use GoHighLevel or Calendly company calendars for clients. Appointments are booked instantly with confirmation links sent to the homeowner and then reassigned internally to the right Energy Consultant based on location and appointment type. This keeps the process efficient and the follow-through tight.

But here's the kicker—systems only work when you apply critical thinking and plan for real-life chaos. What if the EC is out sick? The lead double-books? The proposal isn't prepped in time? You need to anticipate breakdowns, rehearse responses, and pressure-test your process. Because let's be real: good lead partners are gold. You can't afford to burn relationships just because your team missed a step. Own the whole story.

3. CRM Integration Issues

High-quality lead programs provide API ingestion into a dealer's CRM. However, most are not bi-directional, meaning:

- Feedback loops to lead providers must be handled manually.
- Returns and lead performance tracking become difficult to manage.

⚠️ **ANNA'S TIP**

Ask if the provider offers API ingestion and a process for failed leads. What is the backup? Even with leads going directly into a CRM, it's still recommended that the provider supply a Google Sheet or portal login with a list of posted leads as well as confirm that their system will submit a notification to an email (group) or text when one was received to make sure nothing is missed.

4. Managing Duplicate Leads

Duplicate leads are always a challenge, but the best approach is to ingest them while applying a time-based filter:

- Accept duplicates if they are older than 60 days.
- Reject duplicates under 60 days unless sourced from a different provider.

⚠️ **ANNA'S TIP**

If buying leads from multiple sources, track them carefully to avoid paying for the same lead twice (or more!). Tracking the lead source (previous or last entry) is recommended to create a full picture of the customer's journey. Here is an example of how we do it:

Example Custom Fields CRM Setup for Tracking Lead Sources:

- Primary Lead Source = Most recent lead entry
- Secondary Lead Source = Becomes original source
- Sub-Source = More granular campaign tracking

Customer Journey Steps Example

- A customer first comes in through SolarEdge → Later visits your website and fills out a form → Primary Source = Website Lead, Secondary Source = SolarEdge.

- We also often have a Sub-Source field, which is used to differentiate between types of data from the same company. For example, U.S. marketing group could be the lead source, and then the sub-source could be homeowner _60-90_days.

How Do You Manage Duplicates in General?

Depending on your CRM, managing lead data effectively can be a challenge. Software like Salesforce simplifies this by categorizing data into Contacts (customer's name, email, phone), Accounts (customer's address) and Opportunities (customer's inquiry). This structure allows a single contact to have multiple accounts or opportunities associated with them.

For example, if a customer purchases a solar PV system and later wants to add a battery, that would be a new opportunity under their existing account. If they decide to purchase a PV system for a new property, they remain in the same contact but have a new account with a separate opportunity for the new system. This structure also makes service requests easier to manage and improves customer journey tracking when set up correctly.

In GoHighLevel (GHL), the system can be designed around Objects, making it ideal for managing multiple services such as roofing, solar, tree trimming, and more. Our standard setup for dealers follows a single-contact model, where a customer can have multiple opportunities. To prevent duplicate lead costs and optimize pipeline efficiency, we use rules-based workflows:

- If an opportunity is in any pre-contact stage (before signing) and the lead re-enters the system, we locate the existing opportunity, move it back to "Lead" or "Appointment Requested," update the primary source to the latest ingestion, and move the previous source to the secondary source.

This merges records so the company can track where the customer is in their journey, who they've interacted with, and any previous texts, emails, or calls logged in the system.

- If the opportunity is post-signature, we create a duplicate opportunity with a naming convention that clearly identifies it, such as:

  o Customer Name + Request (e.g., Anna Covert + Storage, Anna Covert + EV).

  o Or appending a number (e.g., Anna Covert 2) to indicate a new inquiry without altering the existing post-sale record. This prevents automation disruptions and avoids confusion in project management, sales, and customer communications.

Never Set & Forget!

You still need a dedicated team member who owns these paid lead providers, ensuring spot checks are in place to prevent double or triple payments for:

- Leads that are already sold
- Leads that are active in the sales process
- Leads that are already engaged in speed-to-lead outreach

Without proper oversight, lead costs can quickly spiral out of control, impacting profitability and efficiency. Don't get sucker punched!

5. Proposal & Third-Party Login Hassles

Many lead providers (especially manufacturers and EPCs) require proposals to be generated in their system, adding:

- Additional software to manage
- Potential training and certification requirements for your sales team

It's important to clarify expectations. If you're required to sell a specific service or product, transparency is key. While you own the lead if you paid for it, be mindful that rejecting these may impact your sit and sale rates, which could ultimately affect your ability to scale lead volume in the future.

This is especially important for beta programs where leads are provided at no cost—in these cases, manufacturers expect trackable sales of their products in exchange for distributing leads. For example, if you receive a free REC lead but end up selling the customer Qcells, that would be unethical. However, if you receive a free Generac lead and the customer requires a SolarEdge Home Energy Hub due to their net metering agreement, that is a justifiable and ethical exception.

To avoid conflicts, ensure you:

✔ Understand program expectations and communicate them clearly to your team

✔ Train your sales team to present the expected solution first

✔ Document reasons when a customer chooses a different solution

✔ Be prepared to justify your rationale if selling an alternative product

By staying proactive and transparent, you can maintain strong relationships with manufacturers, maximize future lead opportunities, and uphold ethical sales practices.

6. Lack of Call Recordings for Warm Transfers

Without recordings of warm transfers or appointment-booked calls, you may struggle with:

• Customers denying they agreed to a meeting

• No proof of call quality

⚠️ **ANNA'S TIP**

Partner with lead providers who make transparency non-negotiable—call recordings should be accessible within 24 hours (or on request without drama), and every lead should pass a clear verification process. That means scrubbing for homeownership, confirming qualifications, and having supervisors actively spot-check before anything hits your queue.

Clarify How Phone Transfers Work

Before committing to any call transfer lead program, make sure you clearly understand the process. Ask the right questions up front:

- Will the provider stay on the line to introduce the homeowner during a warm transfer?

- What happens if no one on your team picks up the call?

- If the call drops mid-transfer, what's the recovery process? If the customer calls back, will they be routed back to you or someone else?

- How long will it take for the customer's full information to appear in your CRM?

I've seen entire programs fall apart over issues like this. For example, a lead might transfer successfully, but the solar company's receptionist or energy consultant receives only a name—no address, phone, or email. Now they must attempt to schedule an appointment with incomplete info, while the customer is left perplexed, believing they have already supplied all necessary details. This leads to frustration and trust starts to fade fast.

Other key questions:

- What qualifying questions are being asked and recorded before the transfer?

- Are detailed notes from the provider passed into your CRM with the lead?

- Are these opportunities properly tagged in your CRM (e.g., "Call Back Request" or "Successful Transfer") so your team knows exactly how to follow up?

Don't wait for problems—test, test, test. Run through real scenarios before you go live. Use automated workflows to track transfer status and response time.

How to Increase Connection Rates

Ask the provider if they can use a dedicated transfer phone number, one your team can save in their phones to reduce missed calls due to spam filtering. Many providers simply pass over the customer's number, but with spam calls at an all-time high, that approach kills pickup rates.

My recommendation? Use a tool like CallRail to add an extra layer of protection (use our affiliate link please[6]! We share our referral commissions to help local nonprofits). For a nominal fee, you can assign a dedicated line to this lead source—one that your entire team can save and recognize. Even better, CallRail can simultaneously ring multiple team members, increasing the chances someone picks up and ensuring no opportunity slips through the cracks.

Bonus: You also get call recordings and tracking data without relying on your lead partner for reports. This makes it easier to verify quality, flag issues, and even request refunds if needed, because now you have the full context of what happened after the transfer. You'll also gain insights into volume, timing, and performance—no guesswork required.

Ensure the Right Team is Handling Transfers

Phone transfers should be routed to setters or a dedicated receptionist, not Energy Consultants (ECs) who may already be in meetings with homeowners. ECs handling live transfers can lead to:

---

6 Solarcoasterbook.com/partners

- ⊘ Missed calls

- ⊘ Poor notetaking

- ⊘ Lost opportunities

By structuring clear lead handoff processes and ensuring proper workflows, you can significantly improve connection rates, lead conversion, and overall efficiency. We'll dive deep in the next chapter on sales processes that move the needle!

Next up, let's talk about one of the best-kept secrets in solar sales: Manufacturer Credits—a powerful benefit most dealers don't even realize they can leverage.

What are Manufacturer Credits?

Some manufacturers, like Maxeon, offer traditional dealer programs spearheaded by SunPower that provide credits based on the kilowatts (kW) your company installs. These credits can be used for various products and services, including Covert Communication!

Key Considerations:

- **Expiration:** Credits don't last forever. Depending on your dealer status (Authorized, Silver, Gold, etc.), they may expire semi-annually.

- **Usage:** While some manufacturers offer flexible credit usage, others limit credits to SWAG and company-controlled programs.

⚠ **ANNA'S TIP**

Always Ask! Even if there's no formal program in place, many manufacturers are willing to support co-marketing efforts.

For example:

- REC and SolarEdge have both partnered with my dealers on direct mail campaigns.

- Greentech Renewables and Qcells have supported promotional initiatives in the past.

- Many racking, inverter, storage, and EV charging companies are eager to expand their distribution and may offer rebates, co-marketing, or incentives you're unaware of—but you have to know who and how to ask.

How to Ask for Manufacturer Support

When I start working with a new solar company, I make note of all the manufacturing partners they mention. Then, I ask for an introduction to someone in marketing using this hook:

"We'd like to request brand guidelines and access to approved lifestyle images or videos to share with our customers."

Once I'm connected with the right department, I follow up by asking:

- What dealer programs are currently available?

- If none exist, can we work together to build one?

What Manufacturers Offer Lead Programs?

Manufacturer-sponsored lead programs can be a powerful resource—when they're done right. Some are fully funded, others operate as paid programs with minimal support, and many are short-term pilots or beta tests. The biggest challenge? These programs are constantly evolving, and there's little consistency across providers.

That's why I've created a dedicated resource to help you stay informed at **SolarCoasterBook.com** and update the site regularly with what we learn from the field—program summaries, tips, interviews with industry leaders, and new podcast episodes. As new opportunities and programs emerge or evolve, so will our resources.

I reached out to quite a few manufacturers while writing this—some eagerly shared insights, others... well, crickets. If you're a manufacturer or EPC with a lead program you'd like featured, the invitation is always open.

Here's a snapshot of what was available at the time of writing this book:

- **Maxeon**: Free beta program for Gold Installers
- **REC**: Free beta program for Gold Installers by invitation
- **SunPower by Complete Solar**: Paid program
- **Axia by Qcells**: Paid program
- **SolarEdge**: Paid program, free in some underserved markets
- **SPAN**: Free beta program
- **Duracell**: Free beta program
- **Panasonic**: Previously had a dealer credit system similar to SunPower's, but it was discontinued in late 2024. No formal replacement has been announced yet, though the brand has historically supported co-branded dealer initiatives.
- **Enphase**: Free for approved installers but recently (in 2025) a paid program has been launched in some markets.
- **GAF Energy**: Free program
- **Sol-Ark**: Free program
- **Canadian Solar, SEG, Silfab**: No known lead programs as of now
- **Tesla**: No official PV/storage program, though some dealers do receive leads, and we hear something is in the works. For Tesla Roof, there is a formal paid lead program.
- **Generac**: In the process of developing some type of program including leads and dealer credits.
- **Aurora (software)**: Beta lead program, dealer pays based on contract signed

To understand what makes a manufacturer-led lead program truly work, you need to hear from the builders. In the next two interviews, solar veterans Erick Frazier and Hannah Raines share how they're leading from the front—reimagining what manufacturer programs can become and paving the way for a stronger, smarter dealer ecosystem.

Let's start with Erick.

How to Build a Lead Engine That Scales

Getting leads has always been the first—and most persistent—problem for solar dealers. If you want to understand what it takes to solve that problem at scale, Erick Frazier is the person to learn from. I first met Erick during his rise at SunPower, where he advanced to Director of Demand Generation and played a key role in building one of the most successful dealer-driven lead engines in residential solar.

He didn't stop there. At SolarEdge, Erick built the manufacturer's first-ever lead program in under a year—creating the digital infrastructure, routing logic, and dealer systems from scratch. It was fast, focused, and foundational.

Now? He's joined Tesla. Details are still under wraps, but if history is any indication, whatever he's building next will raise the bar, again!

I sat down with Erick to unpack exactly how he's built these programs from the ground up, what most manufacturers get wrong about lead generation, and what it really takes to create a system that scales.

CASE STUDY: BUILDING THE BLUEPRINT FOR MANUFACTURER-LED GROWTH

Anna: Erick, you've been in solar for a long time—but you didn't start there. What brought you into the industry?

Erick: I was living in China, surrounded by smog, and thought, *I don't want the U.S. to end up like this.* I started researching renewables—wind, geothermal, even podcasts—and eventually landed on solar.

When I got back to the States, I moved to Texas and was so eager to break into the industry that I offered to work for free. That got me into the #1 solar company in the state at the time, Meridian Solar, where I did everything from residential sales to commercial bids. It was hands-on and fast-paced—and it introduced me to SunPower.

Later, I moved to Denver, joined Namasté Solar, and really honed my skills in residential sales. When SunPower opened a Regional Sales Manager role for the Mountain West, I jumped at the opportunity. I already knew the product and now I had the experience to back it up.

Anna: You stepped into that Regional Sales Manager role at a pivotal time. What were you stepping into, and how did the idea for the Master Dealer program first take shape?

Erick: The industry was still young, but SunPower was ready to level up. The challenge we kept running into was scale. We had this incredible brand and product, but solar was still being sold and installed by hundreds of small, local businesses across the country. That fragmentation made it tough to build a consistent national presence.

That's where the idea for the "SunPower by" Master Dealer program came in. We asked ourselves, *what if we could bring brand unity to the field—without owning the whole sales channel?* The goal was to create a top-tier group of dealers who could carry the SunPower name as part of their own. But asking someone to give up their brand identity is no small thing—it's emotional. So, we had to build real value: exclusive access to products, priority support, co-op marketing funds, a VIP hotline, and more.

It started as a pilot with just a few dealers—and by the end, just 8% of our SunPower Dealer partners were driving over 50% of the residential volume through our Master Dealer channel. It turned into one of the most impactful programs I worked on.

Anna: Once the Master Dealer program was in motion, what became the next big focus? What were you seeing in the field?

Erick: Even with the dealer network thriving, one problem never went away: customer acquisition. Every installer was asking the same question—*How do I get more qualified leads?* We realized SunPower had something unique—a national footprint and the ability to drive demand at scale.

At first, we sent leads out for free. We thought dealers would jump on them, but the reality was, without skin in the game, follow-up was inconsistent. So, we started charging—$25 per lead, then $35. That helped create buy-in, but we knew there was a bigger opportunity if we could go further down the funnel. So, we started building out an internal call center to book appointments on behalf of the dealers. That's when things really started to click.

Anna: So, while the Master Dealer program was taking off, SunPower was also exploring a different path—building a direct-to-consumer channel. What was happening behind the scenes?

Erick: Both were happening at once—we were strengthening the Master Dealer network while SunPower was also building a direct-to-homeowner sales channel. It was a bold move, but expensive. Over time, it became clear the economics didn't work at scale. CAC was too high, and we couldn't match the efficiency of strong local dealers.

When we shut down the direct channel, we didn't scrap the team—we pivoted. That's when the appointment-setting program really took off. We repurposed the internal team to qualify leads and book appointments for dealers. Shifting from competing with dealers to enabling them is what unlocked real scale—and laid the foundation for our lead gen strategy.

Anna: That pivot sounds like a turning point. How did the appointment-setting program evolve from there?

Erick: It started small—just a few agents booking off inbound leads, scheduling a couple of days out without direct access to dealer calendars. It wasn't perfect, but it got us moving. The key was dealer buy-in. Once they realized these weren't raw leads but qualified, scheduled opportunities, they started calling customers immediately. That feedback loop was everything.

As traction grew, we refined the process—added pre-qualification, customized scripts, tracked conversion rates, and tested routing strategies. We brought on third-party call centers to manage volume surges and regional spikes. It became less about booking, more and more about building a system that could learn and scale.

What made it truly work wasn't budget—it was how we *managed* the budget. Unlike static quarterly plans, we built a performance-driven model that let us scale up or down in real time. High-performing dealers got more volume instantly. Slower markets pulled back without waste.

Over five years, we grew from 10,000 warm transfers to over 160,000 booked appointments annually. But the real win? Dealers started building their sales process around the program. That's how we knew it was working.

Time for Change...

After over a decade at SunPower, Erick wasn't actively looking to make a move. He had strong relationships and was proud of what they'd built. But as the culture shifted, he finally asked himself, *What else is out there?*

That's when SolarEdge came into the picture. A leader in hardware, they had the tech—but no lead gen, no dealer support, and no infrastructure. It reminded Erick of SunPower in the early days, but this time, he had a blank slate to build it the way he wished it had been done from the start.

Anna: So, you stepped into SolarEdge with a clean slate. What did you build there, and how did you approach it differently this time around?

Erick: Coming in, I wasn't trying to rebuild SunPower—I was trying to learn from it. At SolarEdge, we had the advantage of starting fresh, without legacy systems or old assumptions weighing things down. So instead of retrofitting a solution, we built a streamlined infrastructure from the ground up.

We launched with a clear CTA on December 28, 2023, developed smart lead routing tied to zip codes, and created a single platform that handled dealer assignments, invoicing, and feedback loops all in one place. That integration made a huge difference. At SunPower, those pieces were built in silos and that caused a lot of friction. Here, everything was purpose-built to support dealers and improve the customer experience from the first touchpoint.

Anna: SolarEdge had always operated as a B2B company. What was it like trying to introduce a direct-to-consumer engagement model inside that kind of culture?

Erick: It was a shift, that's for sure. When your entire business is built around hardware and channel relationships, the idea of directly engaging with homeowners raises a lot of internal resistance. Leadership naturally had concerns: *What's the ROI? Are we built to handle this? Can we control the customer experience?*

The key was redefining the purpose. We weren't launching a profit center—we were building a growth enabler. The goal was to help our dealers close more business, not replace them. We positioned it as a break-even engine that strengthened the ecosystem. That framing helped—but the timing wasn't ideal. The market was tightening, and the appetite for anything that looked like a risk was low. We had to move lean, prove fast, and stay relentlessly focused on dealer value.

Anna: Once the platform was live, how did it perform? Did it meet your expectations?

Erick: From a systems standpoint, absolutely. We built a streamlined, scalable platform with real-time routing, dealer-specific logic, and full performance tracking. It delivered better leads and gave us the data to keep improving. The real challenge came with the human factor—aligning internal teams took more work than expected. That's when I started to realize sometimes the biggest barrier isn't the system—it's the belief in it.

Wrapping Up

Erick Frazier has shown time and again that scalable lead engines are built on clarity, consistency, and a deep understanding of how dealers operate. From SunPower to SolarEdge—and now at Tesla—he's shown that when manufacturers invest in systems that serve both the homeowner and the installer, everyone wins.

But even the best systems can fall flat without alignment, feedback loops, and internal champions to keep them running. As Erick made clear, you need to focus on building trust, driving results, and creating something dealers want to grow with.

His work laid the foundation for what a manufacturer-led lead engine can look like. Now, others are taking that blueprint and pushing it even further.

One of them is Hannah Raines, Marketing Director at REC Group. When REC launched its first-ever lead program, the brand's focus was on redefining what *quality* looks like in a dealer-manufacturer relationship.

Let's hear how she approached it—and why REC's model is setting a new standard.

CASE STUDY: REDEFINING LEAD QUALITY AT THE MANUFACTURER LEVEL

After a decade in solar working across marketing, distribution, and dealer enablement, Hannah Raines joined REC Group in 2021—bringing not just deep industry knowledge but a personal mission to reconnect premium product with premium support. A self-described tree hugger at heart, Hannah's solar journey started with a college internship that sparked a career grounded in purpose.

With early roots at AEE Solar (back when it was part of the original Mainstream Energy trifecta), her experience spans the full arc of solar marketing—from warehouse launches and grassroots campaigns to live streaming Sunrun's IPO from the breakroom with champagne in hand. She's seen the highs, the pivots, and the pressure—and now she's focused on shaping the next chapter of solar: one that's values-aligned, customer-first, and built to last.

In late 2024, as market dynamics shifted and dealer feedback grew louder, Hannah and I began collaborating on what would become REC's first-ever lead distribution program. As someone who's worked with lead systems from every angle—sales orgs, marketing vendors, and manufacturers—I had a clear vision for what the industry needed next. Fortunately, Hannah and the team at REC shared that same commitment: build something that delivers real-world impact for dealers and homeowners alike—something built to last, not just impress.

The result? A dealer-first system built with purpose—one that honors the homeowner's journey, elevates the REC brand, and empowers sales teams with the confidence, clarity, and tools to lead with heart and close with conviction.

Anna: You've been at REC since 2021—but something clearly shifted in the last year. Why now? What's happening at REC that created the momentum for launching something new like this lead program?

Hannah: There's definitely been a shift. Since I joined REC, we've been focused on product innovation—Alpha Pure, TwinPeak 5, N-Peak 3, Alpha Pure 2, and most recently, Alpha Pure-R and Alpha Pro M. We've made big moves on the manufacturing side too, with global expansion that's setting us up for long-term scale.

But even with all that, we kept hearing the same thing from our partners: *We need help with lead flow.* It wasn't that they didn't know how to close— it's that they needed a more direct path to connect with homeowners who already trusted our brand. We realized we had people coming to our site, researching REC panels, and reading reviews—but there was no clear next step for them to connect with a certified installer.

So, the goal became clear: build a program that truly supports our installers—not just one that checks a marketing box.

Anna: And what did that look like in practice? What makes this different from the typical manufacturer approach?

Hannah: We designed it from the ground up with usability in mind. That meant leads would be exclusive—one match per homeowner, no racing to the phone. Each inquiry gets routed to a single REC Certified Solar Professional in their area.

Then we solved for the biggest complaint: update fatigue. Installers are busy. They don't want to log into yet another portal. So, we built in two-way updates via email and text. If they've run the appointment or closed the deal, they can just reply. That keeps the pipeline clean without slowing anyone down.

We also wanted to protect the customer experience—so we mask personal numbers and use branded vanity emails. That keeps everything consistent and aligned with the REC brand while also ensuring we maintain visibility on the opportunity from first touch until it's either closed or clearly marked lost.

Anna: Not every installer thrives in a model like this. Who's the ideal REC partner for this kind of lead flow?

Hannah: The ones who lead with value, not just price. Our most successful dealers are usually smaller to mid-sized companies—teams that know their market, have strong operations, and are focused on trust-building. They're not chasing volume at all costs. They want to sell a great product, stand behind it, and grow the right way.

We make premium products—and that means we're committed to supporting partners who know how to sell on performance, reliability, and long-term value. That's where the real alignment happens.

That's why we pair this lead program with our REC Certified Solar Professional Program. It's not just a badge—it unlocks tools like our 25-year ProTrust labor warranty, and if an installer goes out of business, we step in to make things right. That gives both the installer and the homeowner real peace of mind.

Of course, things happen in this industry—it's part of the solar coaster. But the partners who reach this level tend to be the most resilient. They're built for longevity, and we're proud to stand beside them.

Anna: What's the response been like so far?

Hannah: Dealers are telling us it feels different. They're not getting dumped into a lead pile—they're receiving aligned, high-intent conversations.

It's still early, but what we're building is sticky—because it solves real problems. And most importantly, it respects the dealer's time, the homeowner's trust, and the integrity of the REC brand.

We've already shifted our "Find an Installer" section on the website to support this initiative, which means incoming leads are now routed through the program instead of sending homeowners directly to a long list of partners. As a result, we've got a growing waitlist of dealers eager to join.

While we do plan to scale the program, for now it will remain a private, top-tier channel—reserved for those Gold REC Certified Solar Professionals who are aligned with our values and committed to delivering an exceptional customer experience. Stay tuned—things are evolving quickly, and we're just getting started.

Leading with Purpose and Consistency

After spending time with Hannah and digging into how this program came to life, I walked away with something bigger than a checklist of smart features—I saw a company that truly understands what it means to lead with purpose.

In our full interview, I uncovered even more reasons why REC is setting the pace in today's solar market. From their investment in a new manufacturing plant in India to their unwavering support of nonprofit initiatives like the Honnold Foundation and SEI, it's clear this is about more than just panels—it's a movement rooted in purpose, progress, and long-term impact.

They're focused, intentional, and unapologetically committed to doing things the right way—even if that means saying no to trends that don't align. While others race to expand into storage or slash costs to stay afloat, REC is doubling down on quality, dealer relationships, and long-term trust.

And in an industry known for wild swings and constant reinvention, that kind of consistency is what sets real leaders apart.

What Comes Next

REC's approach is a blueprint. It proves that when manufacturers truly listen to their partners and build programs rooted in trust, transparency, and long-term alignment, the results speak for themselves.

But REC isn't the only one rethinking what lead support can look like.

As the industry continues to evolve, new programs are emerging—some from legacy platforms, others from unexpected players like EV manufacturers and e-commerce giants. From paid performance models to co-branded marketplaces, there's no shortage of options. The key is knowing which opportunities are truly built to support your business and which ones will leave you chasing your tail.

Let's look at what else is out there and what you need to know before jumping in. We'll also hear from a few industry leaders who are stepping up to meet the growing appetite for qualified leads, including Blake Gailey (SunPower by Complete Solar) and Kerstin Mueller (Thryve).

Other Lead Programs Worth Watching

In early 2025, major automakers like Hyundai, Honda, Acura, and Genesis ramped up their home energy offerings in response to Tesla's expanding dominance in the residential space. Many partnered with Electrum.co, a platform built to connect homeowner interest with qualified local installers. Backed by Project Sunroof, the U.S. Department of Energy, and several major utilities, Electrum handles much of the pre-sale work—from homeowner education to proposal coordination. Best of all, installers only pay when a deal closes, making it a low-risk way to tap into EV-driven demand.

A few other emerging players are worth keeping on your radar:

- **Qmerit**: A growing installer network focused on EV charger installs, now branching into full-home electrification.

- **Amazon Home Services**: While still in its early stages, Amazon is expected to scale into solar and energy services via its massive contractor network.

These platforms signal a bigger trend: solar lead generation is moving beyond basic media buys into integrated, ecosystem-driven strategies.

And just to address a request I hear *constantly*—"Can we build the Priceline of solar?" Folks, it's already (kind of) been achieved by EnergySage.

EnergySage is a well-known solar quote marketplace where installers compete for homeowner projects and only pay when deals close—plus a platform participation fee. It's earned recognition for its user-friendly interface, transparent quote comparisons, and solid educational resources, making it a go-to for homeowners starting their solar search.

But not everyone in the industry is cheering. Many installers describe it as "a race to the bottom," comparing it to government bidding where the lowest number wins. Yes, there are ways to upsell through adders and change orders, but that model can feel shady to customers and unsustainable for the contractors doing the installation work. It's reminiscent of Tesla's direct model: easy for the customer, but priced so low it leaves little room for quality installation execution.

Worse, when early quotes are overly optimistic and require heavy follow-up just to set realistic expectations, it stops being helpful—and starts to feel like gaming the system, which can replace innovation with manipulation if left unchecked.

But it's not just tech platforms shifting the game. Some EPCs are now launching their own lead programs—focused not on lead lists, but on better sourcing, and real dealer support.

One of the most intriguing transformations I came across was happening at SunPower—now rebranded as SunPower by Complete Solar following its acquisition by Complete Solar. I spoke with Blake Gailey, VP of New Home Sales, who spent over six years at SunPower helping shape the third-party and builder channels. I worked closely with Blake for several years on the dealer program after Paul Sullivan's departure in 2019, so it was especially rewarding to see him return to the ecosystem with even more experience and perspective. After leaving SunPower to join Solaria in 2022, which later merged with Complete Solar and went public in July 2023 as Complete Solaria—it's been a true solar coaster saga. And now, he's back where it all began, bringing it full circle. His breakdown of their strategy revealed just how much had changed—and why it matters.

The new approach centered around three core channels: new home construction, their internal Blue Raven sales team, and a reimagined non-installing dealer (ND) network. With 170 builder relationships, the new homes division was laser-focused on hitting construction timelines.

Meanwhile, Blue Raven provided scale with over 2,000 active reps, and the dealer network was being rebuilt from the ground up.

Blake was candid: "We're bringing back a dealer-first model that's transparent, scalable, and built for long-term success. Dealers want fair margins, ownership, and dependable fulfillment—and we've learned from past mistakes."

Rather than building a massive in-house marketing engine, the team planned to partner with best-in-class demand generation firms and lean on Blue Raven's infrastructure where it made sense. Dealers will get leads—as well as operational support, tech tools, and training to close them.

But here's the twist: Blake is no longer with the company, and despite the direction originally shared, SunPower by Complete Solar has now launched a nationwide leads campaign. It's a sharp pivot—and a perfect reminder of how quickly strategies can shift in the solar coaster.

The truth is, the SunPower of tomorrow won't look anything like the SunPower of the past. Whether they can stay cash-positive and dealer-friendly remains to be seen—but I'll be watching closely.

Another company making moves in this space is Thryve, a newer ECP platform built to be agile, dealer-first, and refreshingly un-corporate. After testing a few appointments through their system and connecting with the team, I spoke with Kerstin Mueller, another SunPower veteran to learn more.

She was clear: Thryve isn't just another lead-gen shop. "We offer appointments if dealers want them, but our focus is on empowering partners to grow—not flooding them with low-quality leads."

What makes Thryve stand out is its structure. They've partnered with GoodLeap for financing, developed a competitive TPO product, and built a quoting and ordering platform that removes friction from the process—down to issuing M1 payments in as little as 48 hours. Their matchmaking system also helps align installers and dealers based on capacity and geographic fit.

Perhaps most importantly, Kerstin emphasized that Thryve treats dealers like partners—not vendors. There's no heavy-handed loyalty requirement or top-down mandates. Just support, flexibility, and a clear understanding of what today's solar pros need to scale.

But while leads are flowing and Thryve has been transparent that the program isn't built to generate revenue—rather, to help dealers grow—the early results have been mixed. Some dealers report low sit and close rates, raising concerns about lead quality, follow-through, and long-term viability.

Adding another layer: the program is being managed by Optimus Platform Services, the same team behind the lead program recently launched for Axia by Qcells.

Is that a red flag? Maybe. It's certainly a data point worth watching. In a space where dealer trust is everything, recycling teams and tactics without clear improvements can leave gaps that need to be filled.

And let's be honest—the entire industry is feeling the squeeze. With utility rates soaring, policy shifts reshaping the landscape, and consumer hesitation at a high, the rules have changed. Lead generation alone isn't enough—what matters now is confidence, value, and dealer support that can stand steady in a volatile market.

That said, one thing is clear: they are delivering appointments—which is more than many others in the space can say right now.

As we'll explore later in this book, lead flow alone won't be enough. In a market this tough, success comes down to one thing: the ability to sell. Only the sharpest sales strategies will cut through.

Other Lead Program Veterans

Not a day goes by without a new LinkedIn DM or email from a lead provider claiming they have *more leads than they know what to do with.* Sound too good to be true? That's because it usually is.

The reality is that most of these players are just here to grab a slice of the pie. Just like we've seen in past incentive spikes, the vultures descend quickly—and right now, it's happening at rocket speed.

I've worked with nearly every provider worth testing: SolarReviews, QuinStreet/Modernize, Clean Energy Experts, Energy Bill Cruncher,

GreenWatt, US Marketing Group, Solar Direct Marketing, Solar Exclusive, ConsumerAffairs, BlueInk Digital, HomeSolarPros, Angi, Lead Genesis, FiveStrata, etc. — the list goes on and on and on and on…

As I've said before, I'm not here to recommend or bash specific providers. My goal is to equip you with the right tools and questions so you can make informed decisions about where to place your trust and your budget.

The variety of lead programs out there may seem tempting, but here's what you really need to consider: how are those leads being generated? This single question often separates scalable success from pipeline burnout.

Most of these platforms rely on digital marketing—SEO arbitrage, paid search, and third-party publisher exchange reseller deals—to drive traffic. But what most haven't acknowledged is that this space is riddled with fraud. Bots, click farms and fake form fills are eroding lead quality at the source.

Meaning that by the time that lead lands in your CRM, it's often older, colder, and barely qualified—if it's even real. And with digital fraud on the rise, adding bad data to the problem of bad leads, the entire industry is feeling the pinch. Time is money. Don't waste it chasing dead ends.

Here's a reminder of the questions you'll want to ask:

- How fresh is the lead, and how are they generating them?
- What are the pricing options and filters?
- How is it delivered, and will it integrate with your CRM?
- What is the return policy?
- Are they honoring consumer privacy rules and regulations?

Your pipeline—and your team's sanity—deserve better!

Final Thoughts on Paid Lead Programs

Paid leads can be highly profitable, or a complete waste of money, depending on how they're managed. Just like caring for a baby, they require constant attention and monitoring. The landscape shifts fast—lead sources are often seasonal, and performance can change overnight due to bad press, regulatory changes, or broader sentiment about the industry. Take your eye off the ball, and what once worked can quickly turn into a costly mistake.

Key Takeaways for Success:

- ✔ Choose lead providers wisely—demand transparency on sourcing and quality.

- ✔ Monitor lead quality and provide real-time feedback—bad leads? Flag them fast.

- ✔ Optimize your speed-to-lead, warm transfer, and CRM setup—seconds matter.

- ✔ Avoid take-all models—only pay for leads that meet your criteria.

From what I've seen—both firsthand and in the data—manufacturer leads often outperform traditional lead vendors. Even when paid, they tend to come with higher intent and better alignment. And when you're lucky enough to be part of a beta program where the leads are free? Even better. Just make sure you're a good partner: responsive, honest, and committed. These programs only work when both sides are invested.

Bottom line: If you're spending on leads, someone needs to own that channel—tracking performance, submitting returns, and constantly refining your strategy. Without clear ownership, you're flying blind.

Or hey—for all you installers out there, here's an idea: maybe you don't sell at all. Join an EPC network, let experienced sales teams bring in the deals, and focus on what you're great at: fulfilling the work and building clean, quality systems. There's more than one way to win in solar and knowing your strengths is part of playing smart.

But for those of you who want to do it all—build your own pipeline, manage your own team, and scale the whole machine—don't worry. We'll break down how to structure it right in Chapter 5.

In the next chapter, we'll move from lead flow to sales flow—exploring what it really means to build a scalable, trustworthy sales engine. From closing strategies to spotting the shady stuff that's hurting the industry, we'll show you how to win business the right way and stay in business long after the others flame out.

CHAPTER 3:

SOLAR SALES STRATEGIES— THE GOOD, THE BAD, AND THE SUPER SHADY

At this point, you know how to get leads. The real question is, can you close them?

I've seen millions of dollars in high-intent leads go to waste—not because the leads weren't qualified, but because the companies chasing them had no sales structure, no accountability, and no clarity on what kind of experience they wanted to deliver. Deals slipped through the cracks. Reps used outdated scripts. Follow-ups fell off. Leadership shrugged, blamed marketing, or doubled down on more leads, hoping volume would cover the gaps. It won't.

Before you worry about CRMs or follow-up cadences, ask yourself: What kind of company are you building? Do you believe in education or urgency? Consultation or conversion? How do you want your customers to *feel* after meeting your team?

There's no one-size-fits-all answer—but there is a right answer for your brand. Get clear on what you stand for, communicate it across your entire team, and build a sales strategy that reinforces it with consistency and trust. In the upcoming chapters, we'll help you find that strategy.

We're diving into hard selling, soft selling, and the hybrid approach— what works, what burns trust, and how to find your edge. We'll also pull back the curtain on some of the shadier "solar bro" tactics still floating around the industry—not to give you ideas, but so you know what to avoid and what your customers may already be wary of.

Ready to define your sales identity and turn opportunity into real revenue? Let's go!

Choosing Your Sales Strategy: Where Do You Stand?

Strong brands have a distinct style. They feel familiar and trustworthy and that comes down to tone of voice and clear value propositions. The way you guide a customer through the decision-making process speaks volumes about your company's values, culture, and long-term vision.

Some teams lean into urgency, pushing for quick commitments. Others focus on education and relationship-building, giving the customer time and space. Most successful organizations find a rhythm somewhere in between.

The key is choosing a strategy that fits your team and the experience you want every customer to walk away with.

In this section, we'll explore the three core sales styles—hard selling, soft selling, and the hybrid approach—so you can determine what works best for your business. Then we'll dig into some cautionary tales from the field to help you avoid the traps that erode trust and hurt performance.

Hard Selling—This is the aggressive, high-pressure approach where sales-people push customers to make a decision immediately. It often includes urgency tactics (e.g., "*This deal is only available today!*"), strong persuasion, and overcoming objections quickly to close the sale.

- **When to Use:** If there is a real need for this urgency, such as a deadline for the ITC solar tax credit or a utility buyback rate decreasing. Waiting could then potentially cost the customer big bucks, and to Michael O'Donnell's (MOD's) point, with a powerful clock ticking, a salesman should not be wasting valuable time on someone who didn't get the memo. You move on to the next opportunity with the goal to reach as many people as possible to help them receive the greatest value.

- **Risks of Hard Selling**: This can feel pushy and might lead to buyer's remorse, which results in cancellations and hard feelings.

Soft Selling—This is the more relaxed, consultative approach that focuses on relationship-building, education, and allowing the customer to make a decision at their own pace. It prioritizes trust, long-term engagement, and providing value without heavy pressure.

- **When to Use:** This strategy is best when dealing with highly analytical buyers who need time to process or have trust concerns. This is also absolutely the right process to deal with referrals and word-of-mouth leads.

- **Risks of Soft Selling**: This can drag out the sales cycle if there is no real urgency, and that might also put you at risk of losing the customer to a competitor who closes faster.

The Hybrid Approach — This is a combo and my personal recommendation to create the best solar sales experience. This focuses on educating the customer while also creating a sense of urgency without overwhelming them. This strategy means ECs must understand when to apply pressure and when to take a step back.

1. **Start with Soft Selling**—Educate, qualify, and build rapport.

2. **Introduce Urgency**—Use hard sell tactics strategically (e.g., "Solar permits take time—let's lock in your spot.").

3. **Guide the Customer**—Support their decision-making process without applying pressure. People are far more likely to commit when they feel in control and even more so when subtle psychological cues are working with their instincts, not against them. I'll break down exactly how I use behavioral science to guide that process (without the gimmicks) in the next chapter—so hang tight!

A Cautionary Tale: When Sales Strategy Crosses the Line

Let's be clear: there's nothing wrong with selling confidently or closing on the first visit—as long as it's done ethically, with respect for the customer's autonomy and trust. But too often, solar companies swing too far in one direction, implementing rigid or manipulative tactics that backfire in the long run.

The One-Visit Close Gone Wrong

At one company, sales reps were forced into a strict *one-visit close* model. If the customer didn't sign that day, the rep lost the lead, and it was reassigned to a manager who took over and applied even more pressure for the customer to close.

The impact?

- Reps were stressed and desperate, leading to rushed and aggressive pitches.

- Customers felt blindsided and distrustful. "*Why is someone else suddenly calling me? What happened to the rep I just met?*"

- Deals closed under pressure were more likely to cancel, leaving a trail of churn and bad reviews.

This kind of culture creates burnout, resentment, and reputation damage. And perhaps most ironically, it trains reps to value quantity over quality—rushing to close at the expense of building a real connection.

The 7-Day Cutoff that Undermined Everything

Another company implemented a policy: if a deal wasn't closed within seven business days, the sales manager would follow up with a lower offer—cutting the rep out and using their lost commission as the "discount."

This might boost short-term conversions, but the long-term damage was massive:

- Customers learned to wait (referrals and reviews reinforced this). They'd stall just to get the better deal.

- Reps lost trust in their own company and started taking shortcuts just to avoid being cut out.

- The brand became associated with bait-and-switch tactics and discounts that devalued the entire product offering.

It's a classic case of cutting off your nose to spite your face—leadership ended up working against their own team. Instead of empowering reps to close smartly and authentically, they undermined them and trained customers to delay. That said, recycling leads after a period of inactivity can still be a highly effective strategy when done right.

Assigning a specific team to re-engage cold leads is smart, especially once the original rep stops hearing back. But it doesn't have to be slimy. A well-trained team can simply find out why the process stalled. If price was the issue, they can introduce a new incentive or rebate—gathering intel while protecting the team.

This approach also works well for customers disqualified due to credit. Credit scores change, and reaching out down the line shows you care about their journey. It builds trust, reinforces your brand, and may turn a lost lead into a loyal customer.

Go a step further and build this strategy into a targeted campaign—with drip email messaging that shares tips for improving credit, updates on new programs, and other ways the consumer can stay engaged with your brand (referrals, community fundraisers, etc.). Don't wait for them to become qualified; nurture the relationship and stay top of mind until the timing is right.

> ⚠️ **ANNA'S TIP**
>
> Make it clear to your team—updating the CRM is the only way to protect a lead. Say an EC meets with a homeowner, presents a proposal, and the customer says they're leaving for vacation and to follow up in three weeks. That's valid. These are what I call LIMBO leads—not lost, just paused. As long as the EC logs clear notes and sets tasks to follow up, the lead stays theirs. But if they treat LIMBO as a parking lot—no updates, no effort—it'll show up in the data.

Trust Takes Time—But Timing Still Matters

On the other end of the spectrum, some companies go too soft—banning first-visit closes altogether. Their reasoning? *"We want to give customers time to think."*

That might sound noble, but here's the truth: sometimes the customer is ready. They've done their homework. They trust the rep. They're excited about the solution. Forcing them to wait introduces unnecessary friction and doubt and opens the door for a competitor to step in.

It's like telling someone who's ready to join the gym, "Come back next week, and we'll let you sign up."

I don't believe in pushing people, but I do believe in meeting them where they are. If someone is confident, informed, and ready to move forward, we should honor that momentum, not interrupt it.

That said, not everyone sees it that way.

Scott Aronson, CEO of SunRev Inc., is one of the most trusted professionals I know in the solar industry, and he doesn't believe in first visit closes at all. While I don't necessarily agree, I respect his approach deeply.

He's built a highly successful business grounded in transparency, patience, and customer trust.

It's not that he never lets a customer sign on the first visit—but it's rare. The only time he makes that exception is when the homeowner has already met with multiple solar companies and is clearly ready to make an informed decision.

I sat down with Scott to hear his side of the story and learn how he's turned that philosophy into a solar sales machine. His results speak for themselves, and his approach just might challenge your assumptions about what it takes to win in this industry.

CASE STUDY: BUILDING CUSTOMER LOYALTY ONE HONEST ANSWER AT A TIME

Scott Aronson isn't your average solar CEO. After nearly 20 years at the Better Business Bureau—five of those as Vice President—he's brought a customer-first philosophy to solar sales, and it's paying off. In a market crowded with confusion and half-truths, Scott and his team at SunRev are leading with radical transparency.

When I first met Scott, he was an elite SunPower dealer with impressive stats, running a high-performing virtual sales model focused on California and Nevada. Since then, he's transitioned into the Powur network and partnered with other EPCs—but his vision has remained consistent: prioritize trust, educate the customer, and never pressure the sale.

While many in the industry chase the one-call close, SunRev proudly takes a different approach. They don't allow customers to sign on the first visit—not because they're holding back, but because they believe trust is earned through transparency, not pressure.

And it's working. With a sit rate over 80%, SunRev's team doesn't just wait for the second meeting—they earn it by tackling five critical questions most solar companies won't even touch. By being upfront from the start, they create credibility, curiosity, and a reason for homeowners to come back. What are those five topics, you ask?

1. What's the real difference between solar panel warranties—and why does it matter who you buy from?

2. How does battery storage really work under NEM 3.0 —and what happens if there's a blackout during peak hours?

3. How long will your battery last—and how much will it cost to replace it?

4. What will it cost to remove and reinstall your solar panels when you replace your roof?

5. How do low-interest solar loans really work—and what will you owe if you sell your home early?

Most leading solar companies will answer questions 1 and 2 without hesitation—but the others came as a surprise to me. Let's take a closer look at each of those unique questions—the answers might just surprise you, starting with battery life (don't worry, you can read the full interview online).

Battery Replacement: The Conversation No One Wants to Have

Anna: Most reps avoid talking about battery replacement—but you bring it up early. Why is that such an important part of your sales conversation?
Scott: It comes down to fear. Most reps worry that if they mention any future cost, especially something like battery replacement, they'll scare off the sale. But that's short-term thinking—and it's exactly why so many homeowners end up blindsided later.

The truth is that your battery will need to be replaced in about 15 years. If you paid cash or financed the system, that replacement isn't included—it'll be out-of-pocket. And if no one tells you that upfront? That's misleading.

So, we bring it up early: *"This battery will save you money, but it won't last forever. Here's what a replacement would cost today. Let's factor that into your financial plan now."*

We're not afraid of that conversation. Honestly, we see it as our responsibility. I'm not in this for a one-time sale—I want to be the person that homeowner calls in 15 years when it's time for a replacement. And they will—because we were honest from day one.

Planning for the Inevitable: Your Roof's Role in Solar

Anna: Roofing can be one of those hidden deal-breakers if it's not addressed early. How do you bring it up in a way that builds trust instead of hesitation?

Scott: It's a huge issue and most reps either ignore it, or gloss over it to keep the deal moving. But here's the truth: if your roof is 15 years old and your panels are built to last 30, you're almost guaranteed to face a reroof during the system's life. And removing and reinstalling panels? That can cost around $5,000 today and likely more down the line.

Most reps hear "15-year-old roof" and say, "Perfect!"—then just keep going. We don't do that. We stop and say, *"Let's talk about what happens in 15 years—and how you can prepare now."*

Because if we don't, it's going to be an unwanted surprise later. I always ask, *"Did any other company bring this up?"* The answer is almost always no—and that's when the customer realizes who's really looking out for them. We're not chasing quick closes. We're thinking 10, 20, 30 years ahead. That's how you earn trust, win the deal, and keep the relationship.

The Financing Game—What APR Doesn't Tell You

Anna: Loans used to be a clear win for homeowners when interest rates were low—but the landscape has changed. What's your take on how financing is being sold today?

Scott: A few years ago, solar loans were unbeatable. You could get 0.99% or 1.99% rates all day, and at those numbers, loans were a fantastic deal. But that era is over. Interest rates have climbed, and too many reps are still pushing 3.99% loans without explaining what those actually cost.

Here's the truth: that "low APR" loan isn't free money. To advertise 3.99%, lenders buy down the rate from 11–12% by inflating the loan amount upfront—sometimes adding $20,000 or more to the principal. A $37,000 net system can suddenly look like $61,000 on paper. The monthly payment drops, but the payoff math tells a different story. Here's how we break it down for the consumer:

Loan Comparison Example: Understanding APR and Loan Terms

When financing a solar system, the structure of the loan changes both monthly payments and the balance if paid off early. Below is a real-world comparison:

Loan Option	Term	APR	Loan Amount	Monthly Payment	Early Payoff Impact
Option 1	25 Yrs	11.99%	$37,428	$427.60	Balance aligns with principal
Option 2	25 Yrs	3.99%	$61,636	$337.00	Higher payoff due to inflated principal

Key Takeaways:

- The higher-APR loan matches the system's actual cost, so the payoff balance is straightforward.
- The lower-APR loan looks cheaper monthly, but includes ~$24,000 in extra principal to buy down the rate.
- If the loan runs full term, the 3.99% option can save money—but if paid off early, the inflated balance is a costly surprise.

Scott (continued): This is the kind of financial trap homeowners walk into every day and no one's warning them. We are.

That's why I ask every customer, *"Are you planning to move in the next 8 years?"* Because if they are, that shiny 3.99% APR could be the most expensive mistake they ever make. We walk them through the real math—not a sales pitch. I'm not here to close a deal—I'm here to make sure they don't get burned.

If a rep can't explain financing—or worse, hides it—they have no business selling solar. Our job is to protect the customer, not bury them in a loan they'll regret.

We're not afraid to slow the sale down. Because when homeowners see the full financial picture, they choose the company that told them the truth.

Final Thoughts: Truth, Transparency, and the SunRev Difference

Scott Aronson built SunRev on one core belief: honesty is the ultimate closing tool. He doesn't believe in high-pressure sales—he believes in education. By challenging assumptions, calling out shortcuts, and leading with radical transparency, Scott earns what others try to force: trust.

As he puts it, *"When we slow down, show the math, and speak the truth—people pay attention."*

At SunRev, they don't sell—they educate. If a homeowner met with Tesla, Scott will ask, *"Let me guess—you got a 20-second call with zero details?"* Sunrun? *"Did they push a PPA without explaining what ownership really means?"*

They know the game. They know the script. And by breaking it—with clarity, not pressure—they stand out.

Instead of pushing for the close, Scott invites the customer to reflect. He simply asks, *"Did the other companies tell you all this?"* Nine times out of ten, the answer is no.

That moment earns the second meeting—not through urgency, but through trust. The result? Fewer cancellations, stronger relationships, and customers who come back again and again.

What's Next

Now that we've heard from both sides of the fence—MOD's urgency-driven hard selling and Scott's transparency-first soft selling—it's time to pause before we land in the middle.

Because somewhere between those two approaches lies a darker force at play: **the shady side of solar sales**. You've seen the ads, heard the horror stories, maybe even inherited the mess left behind by a bad actor. These are cracks in the foundation of an industry that desperately needs public trust.

I've seen two types of people rise in solar: those who use their powers for good—educating, empowering, and guiding customers with integrity—and those who chase short-term profit with zero accountability. Think *Return of the Jedi*—you can take the high road and become a trusted guide, or you can be seduced by the dark side, using manipulation and pressure to hit your numbers at any cost.

Before we dive into the hybrid model, we need to shine a light on what not to do—so you can avoid it, protect your brand, and make sure your team never crosses that line. We'll also take a moment to highlight some of the real heroes out there—people and companies pushing for better standards and doing it right.

The Shady Side of Solar Sales

One of the biggest threats to solar comes from inside the house—cue the "Solar Bros." These smooth-talking reps inflate system performance, twist proposal numbers, and chase commissions at the expense of customer trust. And every time they do, the whole industry pays for it.

> *"Look, there's no denying it—we've still got a "solar bro" problem in some corners of the industry. Overselling, underdelivering, bait-and-switch tactics...it gives the whole sector a black eye. And it's frustrating, because there are so many good companies out there doing it right."*
>
> – Erick Frazier, Solar Demand Gen Specialist since 2009

A common scam involves designing a system incorrectly—showing a 100% offset on a utility bill, even when the panels are installed on multiple roofs, not all south-facing. This distorts production estimates, making the system appear cheaper than a true 100% offset system. The homeowner believes they're eliminating their utility bill, only to discover once the system is commissioned that they still owe a balance to their power company, on top of their solar loan, lease or PPA payment. This example is common, but let's talk about how, when unchecked, it can get wildly out of control using this case study from Tarek Azar founder of District Energy LLC, a client of mine located in the District of Columbia.

CASE STUDY: THE HIGH COST OF INFLATED PRODUCTION CLAIMS

Anna: Tarek, you've been installing solar in one of the most unique and challenging environments in the country—historic Washington, D.C. But what really caught my attention when we first spoke was the fraud story you shared. Can you walk us through what happened?

Tarek: Sure. D.C.'s SREC program was designed to reward homeowners for clean energy production, and for years, it ran on good faith. Systems under 10 kW didn't require revenue-grade meters—estimates were accepted. Most installers were honest, but a few bad actors exploited that system. They'd claim systems were perfectly pitched and south-facing when, in reality, panels were installed on multiple roof surfaces—including east- and even north-facing ones.

Anna: And by inflating the performance numbers, they were able to claim more SRECs than the system was truly producing?

Tarek: Exactly. These companies submitted falsified specs and cashed in on overestimated production. One lawsuit even alleged that nearly $8 million in excess credits were claimed through this kind of manipulation. And here's the kicker—the homeowners had no idea. They trusted their installer. But when the system didn't perform and SREC regulators started investigating, the homeowners were the ones left holding the bag.

Anna: That's infuriating. And now honest customers are being penalized?

Tarek: Unfortunately, yes. In response to the fraud, the D.C. Public Service Commission passed a rule requiring revenue-grade meters for systems under 10 kW. Homeowners now must pay $500–$600 for revenue-graded meters to stay compliant—or they lose their SREC income. These are people who followed the rules, and now they're being punished for someone else's deception.

Anna: It's a perfect example of how bad actors don't just hurt the industry—they hurt *everyone*. What are the biggest lessons here?

Tarek: Transparency is everything. Homeowners deserve to know exactly how their system is designed, what it's projected to produce, and how the financials really work, without hype.

We also need smarter regulations that target the real problem, not blanket penalties that end up hurting honest homeowners. And most importantly, solar companies need to educate, not just sell. Customers should understand how things like SRECs are calculated, what they're worth, and what rights they have. There are good actors out there (like us) truly offering 100% no-cost solar, designed to maximize electric energy production, long-term savings, and system value. No hidden strings, no inflated projections. Just real production, real savings, and real accountability. However, these programs will be at risk if the ITC tax credits disappear under the new legislation, as the 30% is currently used to fund the cost of the equipment.

To Conclude

In 2025 District Energy launched its "no-cost solar program" and set a new standard. In the aftermath of widespread deception, they chose transparency over shortcuts and education over exploitation. Their response is a model for how this industry *should* operate—with integrity, clarity, and a long-term commitment to doing what's right. The question is—are you?

When the Site Just Doesn't Pencil Out

This shouldn't be a shocker, sometimes solar just isn't a great fit for the site. And that's not a failure of the tech or the sales process. It's reality.

Shading is the most common reason a system underdelivers. Trees, chimneys, neighboring buildings, and seasonal sun angles all matter. A good designer can work around some of it with panel-level optimization and smart placement—but not every site is worth the effort. A home buried in trees in the Pacific Northwest? That's not just bad economics, it's poor ethics to sell it as "green" if it won't offset its own footprint.

Be real with the customer. If they need to cut down half their property or spend more on maintenance than they'll save on power, it's not a good deal. And no, "doing it for the environment" doesn't justify a system that won't perform.

Also, while solar is clean energy, panel production isn't impact-free. If the system won't outperform the grid over its lifetime, you're selling an illusion—not sustainability.

The takeaway? Be honest. Don't fudge numbers or mislead customers about performance. Be realistic about shading, production, and how green their investment really is. Energy independence is valid—but solar isn't the only solution. In some cases, generators offer the same protection with less environmental and financial impact.

Next up, let's address one of the most damaging sales trends in the industry: misrepresenting battery systems. Overselling their capabilities has led to a wave of consumer complaints and unmet expectations. Let's make sure you're not caught up in the mess.

Are You Selling Battery Backup or Energy Storage?

While this seems nuanced, it is a key insight that is often overlooked by even the biggest in the industry. The key difference between battery backup and energy storage comes down to purpose, functionality, and grid interaction. Ask a simple question: "<homeowner>, *what is most important to you, blackout protection, or saving money?*"

"Ask the real question: 'Are you okay if your battery's empty during an outage?' If backup matters, we recommend a second battery—or reset expectations. We're not here to sell a fantasy. When the power goes out, they won't remember the savings—they'll remember who told them the truth."

– Eric Wedell, Energy Plus Solar

Battery Backup—Stand-Alone or Backup Systems

Battery backup is ideal for homeowners whose main concern is staying powered during grid outages. These systems charge from either the grid or solar panels and automatically kick in when the grid goes down, providing short-term emergency power. They're commonly used to keep essential appliances—like lights, refrigerators, or medical devices—running during blackouts, especially in areas with frequent outages or unreliable utility service. However, unless paired with a broader energy management system, battery backups typically don't reduce daily electricity bills.

Energy Storage—Full-Scale Energy Management

Full-scale energy storage is ideal for homeowners who want to maximize their solar investment, reduce electricity bills, and move toward energy independence. These systems store excess energy generated by solar panels—or drawn from the grid—and discharge it strategically during peak demand times or high-rate periods. This approach maximizes solar self-consumption by storing surplus solar energy for use at night, helping homeowners rely less on the grid. While it can also provide backup power like a basic battery system, its primary strength lies in ongoing, intelligent energy management.

The Key Differences at a Glance

Feature	Battery Backup	Energy Storage
Primary Function	Emergency power during outages	Ongoing energy optimization & backup
Works with Solar?	Optional	Yes, often required
Saves Money on Electricity?	No	Yes, through load shifting & self-consumption
Grid-Connected?	Not necessarily	Usually
Use Case	Short-term power supply	Long-term energy management & grid independence

So why does this nuance matter when you're selling a system? Let me introduce you to Ambrose Solar, a long-time client of mine based in Vacaville, California. Ambrose's team are champions of doing solar the *right* way. From day one, they have prioritized education over shortcuts, accuracy over hype, and long-term satisfaction over quick wins. They believe that designing solar + storage systems mean understanding behavior, usage patterns, and policy—not just quoting kilowatts.

It's this level of detail that has positioned them as a leader in the space and with a plethora of referrals to show for it. Their commitment to honest selling and real-world results makes them a perfect example of how integrity and insight can power a stronger, more sustainable industry.

CASE STUDY: PAT W. VS. JOSE A.—GETTING SOLAR + STORAGE RIGHT IN A NEM 3.0 WORLD

Interview with Dayne Litchfield from Ambrose Solar

Anna: Dayne, let's talk about Pat W.—a client who was sold a "100% offset" system that looked good on paper but didn't work for his lifestyle.

Dayne: Yeah, Pat's system technically produced 100.15% of his annual usage, but month-to-month it was totally out of sync. He was underproducing in the winter when he needed energy most and overproducing in the summer—with no battery to store it or strategy to shift his load.

Anna: So basically, he was sold on averages, not actuals.

Dayne: Exactly. His system was designed for the utility spreadsheet, not the real world. It ignored seasonal usage trends, interval data, on-peak pricing, and worst of all—what NEM 3.0 does to your bill if you don't manage your load and storage smartly.

Pat April Usage:

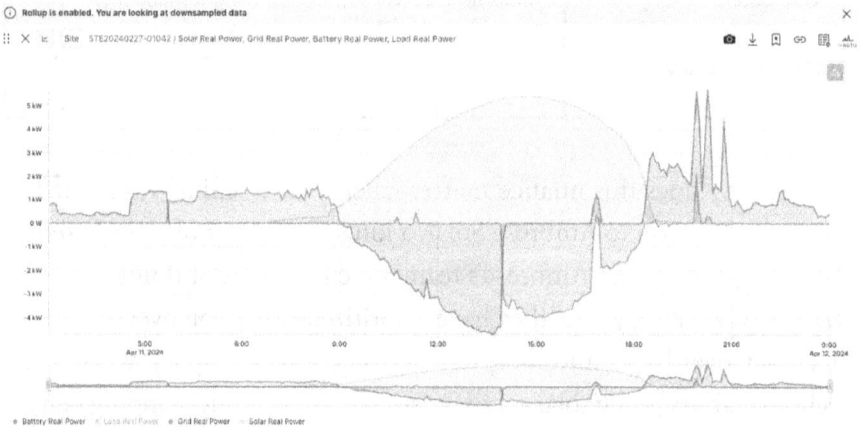

Pat January Usage:

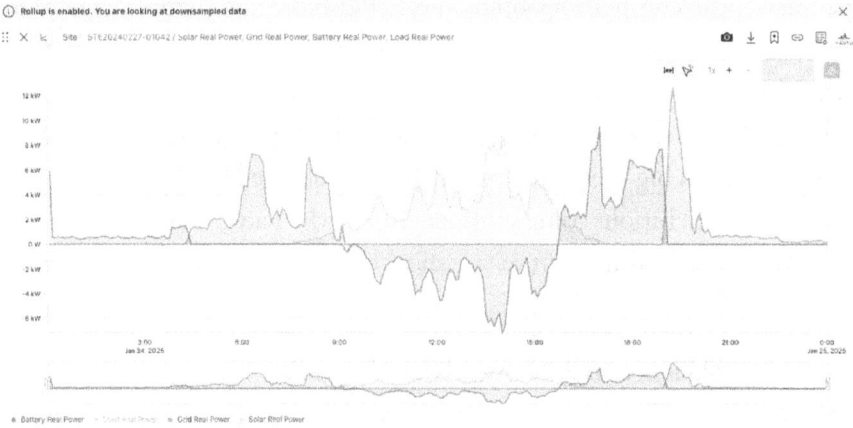

The Interval Data that Told the Truth

Anna: I want to pause here and walk people through how to read interval data. This is precisely why battery sizing can't be based on guesswork—or springtime averages.

Dayne: Right. Here's a good example. This client had a proposal from another company that *did* use interval data—but they totally missed summer usage. And that's a big deal. Most people use way more energy at night in the summer.

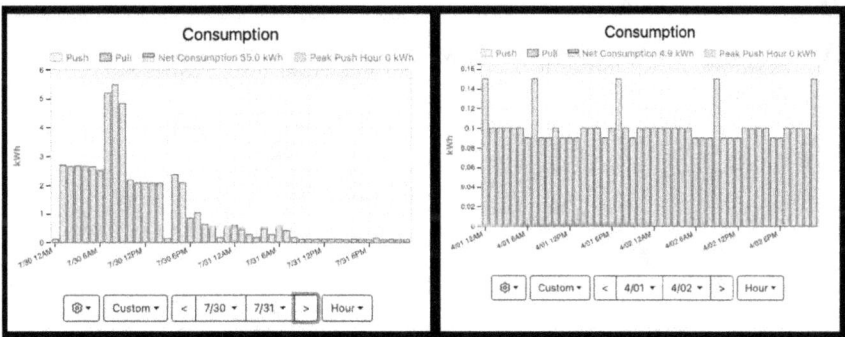

Look at this: in April, the client's nighttime use was only 4.9 kWh. But in July? It spiked to 55 kWh. If you sized the battery based on April, you'd recommend a 5 kWh battery—which would've been a disaster.

This isn't Pat's data, but we used his story to explain it. Our rep wanted to match the competitor's offer, and I told him, fine—but you *have* to show the client Pat's story and explain what's about to happen if they go that route.

We didn't have this level of software when Pat went solar, but we do now—and it makes a big 10x difference! If we had followed that April logic, Pat would've been furious come summer. This is why I always say, Batteries are for the summer. You've got to size them based on peak seasonal demand, not the shoulder months.

Pat's Partial Fix... and the Power Bill to Prove It

Anna: Pat didn't want to change the solar part—just added a battery instead. How'd that go?

Dayne: Predictably bad. After 14 days, he got a $52.16 bill, even though his system was offsetting his annual usage. He was still pulling from the grid at $0.43/kWh and earning just $0.017/kWh for what he exported.

Anna: So, he was paying 25x more to buy power than he was getting to sell it.

Dayne: That's NEM 3.0 in action. Solar alone doesn't cut it anymore—especially when it's misaligned with demand. And battery-only without proper solar support? Equally ineffective.

Meanwhile: Jose A. Did it Right

Anna: Now let's contrast that with Jose A.—who listened from the first meeting.

Yearly Total | Est. solar production: **18,713 kWh** | Home usage: **10,428 kWh**

	JAN	FEB	MAR	APR	MAY	JUN	JUL	AUG	SEP	OCT	NOV	DEC
	729	952	1590	2012	2356	2378	2388	2137	1665	1319	896	673
	802	828	805	809	787	973	978	1017	1001	834	790	803

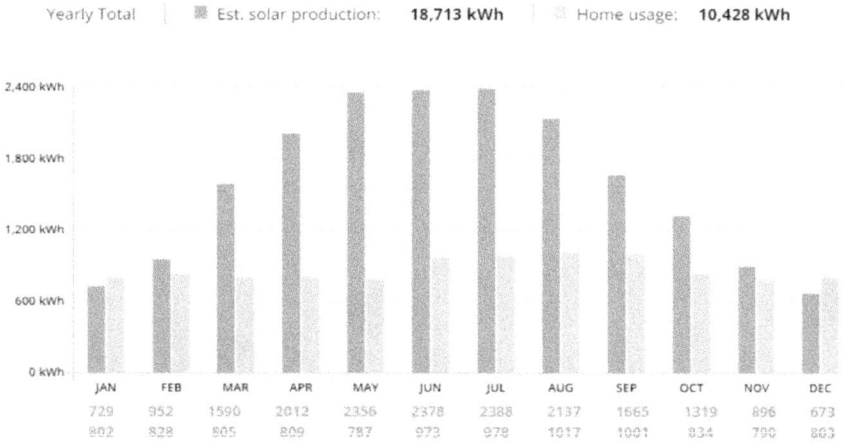

Dayne: Jose let us model his interval data, analyze his usage curve, and design accordingly. He installed:

- **18,713 kWh** solar production
- **10,428 kWh** usage
- **19.5 kWh battery**

Technically, he still pulled 120.564 kWh from the grid, but the system was designed to overproduce during high-yield months. That month, he sent 742+ kWh back and earned $59.43 in credits, nearly matching his usage cost.

Anna: And how was his bill?

Dayne: A credit balance of -$100.42 and no payment due. That over-production was part of the strategy. Jose wanted to build up credits for winter—and that's exactly what the system was designed to do.

Third Time's the Charm

Anna: Pat eventually came back—*again*—right?

Dayne: Third time's the charm. After trying two batteries and no improvement, he finally agreed to install what we originally proposed: the right balance of solar and storage, based on seasonal behavior and interval load. Now? He's happy.

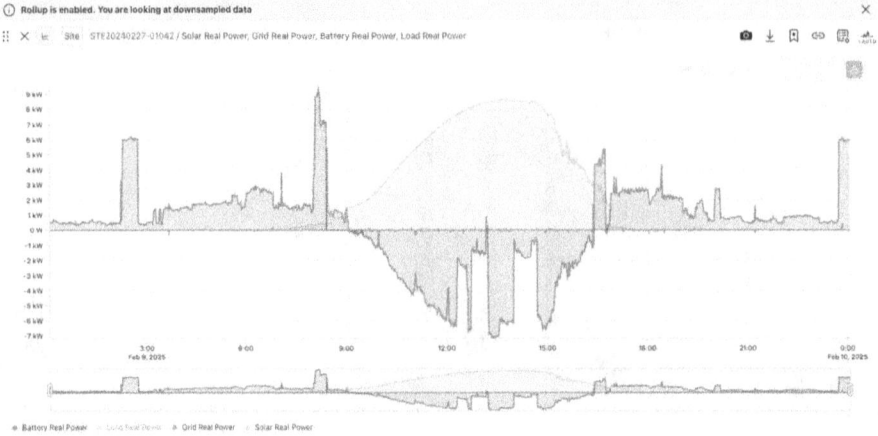

Anna: So, what's the final takeaway?

Dayne: Solar is for the Winter. Batteries are for the Summer. Offset means nothing without alignment. Design the system around the client's behavior, not the utility's incentives. And tell the truth—even if it's harder to sell up front.

Final Thoughts: The Difference Between Good Solar and Fast Solar

Pat bought the hype. Jose trusted the data.

Pat heard a promise. Jose got a plan.

Same goal—very different journeys. And that's the difference between a *solar bro* and a real solar professional.

The best solar companies build long-term energy strategies based on honesty, transparency, and real-world usage. They take the time to analyze interval data, discuss tradeoffs, and design systems that work across seasons and billing structures—not just for the sales chart this month.

When you lead with truth over tactics, something remarkable happens: your customers trust you. They refer you. They come back. And most importantly, their systems actually work. Go team!

But not every company plays by those rules.

Protecting against Fly-by-Night Sellers

We'll close this chapter by looking at one of the biggest threats to homeowner trust: fly-by-night solar sales companies. These outfits flood new markets with aggressive, high-pressure tactics, overpromise on performance, and then disappear—leaving behind unfinished installs, poor workmanship, and homeowners locked into loans they never fully understood.

> *"The dealer model is seductive—a blitz crew rolls into town, promises volume, asks for your lowest redline, and says they'll flood your pipeline. And sure, they might sell 100 jobs. But they don't care about your brand, your process, or your customer. The second a cheaper EPC shows up, they're gone—and you're left cleaning up the wreckage."*
>
> – Justin Nielsen, Wolf River Electric

While solar is an exciting investment, not all sales practices are created equal—and some states are stepping up to protect consumers. In places like Washington and Nevada, solar reps must be W-2 employees of a licensed installer, preventing commission-only reps from making unrealistic promises just to close a sale. California requires a Home Improvement Salesperson (HIS) license, including fingerprinting and background checks, to ensure professionalism and accountability.

Other states—Minnesota, New York, Vermont, and New Mexico—have published homeowner guides to help navigate solar contracts and financing, while Utah and Maryland now mandate upfront disclosure of key system details and financial terms.

These protections are a response to growing reports of misrepresentation and predatory sales tactics. The goal is simple: ensure homeowners get honest, reliable information. But it also raises a bigger industry question—does limiting financing options like leasing help protect consumers, or does it limit access to solar altogether?

Why Washington Took a Stand on Solar Leasing

To dive deeper, I sat down with a longtime client, Howard Lamb, founder of Sunergy Systems and a solar industry veteran with over 30 years of experience. Howard has seen it all—from the early days of solar adoption to the rise of new incentives and evolving regulations. As a founding member of WASEIA (Washington Solar Energy Industries Association), he's been at the forefront of policy discussions that have shaped the state's solar market.

One thing that sets Washington apart? It has never allowed leased solar systems to qualify for production incentives.

I was curious—why has Washington held firm on this policy? Wouldn't leasing help more homeowners go solar? And with rising electricity costs, are consumers getting enough financial flexibility?

Howard had a lot to say, and his insights might surprise you. Here's what I learned.

Anna: Let's talk about Washington. It's one of the few states where solar leasing never took off. Why was that?

Howard: Washington never technically banned solar leases, but when the state launched its incentive program in 2005, it was deliberately structured to benefit homeowners—not third-party leasing companies. The production incentives were paid directly to the homeowner, and with our already low electricity rates, those incentives were what made solar pencil out. Leasing simply didn't make financial sense in that model. But more than that, the goal was to promote ownership, because the state saw solar as more than just bill savings. It was about job creation, supporting local manufacturing, and encouraging long-term investment in renewables. If leasing companies had come in, claimed the incentives, and then left, it would've undermined everything. And let's be honest, most leases only guarantee the system for 10 years. After that, there's no long-term support, no accountability, and no real stake in the community.

Anna: But leases do help people who can't afford to buy, right?

Howard: That's the big debate. Leasing does open the door for more people, but often at the expense of long-term savings. The leasing company keeps the tax credit, the energy credits, and the production incentives.

Homeowners just get the power, and not always the best deal. Washington made a conscious decision: structure the system so homeowners benefit most over time, not just in the moment.

Anna: Tell me more about the incentive program. It sounds like it was pretty unique.

Howard: It was one of the best in the country. Homeowners got paid per kilowatt-hour their system produced and that was on top of standard net metering. But here's the kicker: if you used Washington-made panels or inverters, your incentive payments increased significantly.

- Regular equipment: $0.15 per kWh

- WA-made panels: $0.36 per kWh

- WA-made panels and inverters: $0.54 per kWh

Those checks came annually in Q3, based on your system's production. You had two meters—one for NEM and one for production—so you saved on your bill and got paid for every kilowatt-hour generated, whether you used it or not. A 10 kW system could bring in up to $5,400 a year. It was a great return—too great, actually.

Anna: Too great? What went wrong?

Howard: Some manufacturers saw an opportunity. Companies like Silicon Energy raised their prices 2x–3x, knowing homeowners would still "make it back" through the incentive checks. But the payback took longer, the panels weren't the best quality, and it ended up inflating the market. At the same time, SolarCity was lobbying hard to introduce leasing in Washington.

We'd seen what happened in other states. Leasing companies came in, burned through the incentives, then left when the well dried up—leaving behind stranded customers and local installers struggling to stay afloat. Fast forward: Silicon Energy? Gone. SolarCity? Gone. But the local companies that fought for smarter policies? We're still here.

Anna: So how did the local solar community respond to that challenge?

Howard: A bunch of local installers—including me, A&R Solar, South Sound Solar, Fire Mountain Solar, Puget Sound Solar, Whidbey Sun &

Wind, and Western Solar—banded together and met with legislators. We weren't lobbyists, just small business owners who cared about the industry. We explained that if out-of-state companies were allowed to dominate the market, the incentive funds could be gone in nine months, leaving Washington with nothing to show for it.

Lawmakers listened. They adjusted the program, lowered the bonus for in-state manufacturing, and put guardrails in place to prevent gaming the system. We also had support from some key utility partners who saw the long-term grid benefits of smart solar policy. By working with—not against—utilities, we built something sustainable.

The Power of Industry-Led Change

Washington's solar industry made a deliberate choice—one that kept money in the state, protected homeowners, and ensured long-term sustainability. Rather than following the leasing-driven model that took over in other states, local installers stood up and fought for a better path— one that prioritized homeowner benefits, local jobs, and long-term industry stability.

The biggest takeaway? You have the power to shape policy.

Howard Lamb and a group of committed local installers came together, formed the Solar Association of Washington, and used their collective expertise to advocate for policies that truly benefited homeowners. Over time, their efforts evolved into WASEIA (Washington Solar Energy Industries Association), which united even more in-state installation companies under a single, powerful voice. Because of their leadership, Washington's solar policies were shaped by those who understood the industry best. The people on the ground installing systems, serving homeowners, and driving real energy change.

Now, with solar policies evolving nationwide and net metering changes on the horizon, the industry is at a pivotal moment. The future of solar will be shaped not only by energy storage incentives, smart grid integration, and new ownership models—like community solar and shared system programs—but also by strong partnerships with utilities, cities, and counties working together to modernize the grid and expand equitable access to clean energy.

As these shifts unfold, who will lead the conversation? Will it be local businesses and seasoned experts who truly understand what homeowners need? Or will it be outside interests chasing quick wins, leaving communities to deal with the fallout?

Across the country, the rules are being rewritten. This is the moment to make waves—to influence policy, elevate your voice, and ensure solar remains both sustainable and accessible. The window for action is wide open, so how will you flip the script?

But Washington isn't the only state where local voices shaped solar policy. In California—the country's biggest solar market—the battles have been even fiercer. And one woman has been at the center of it all.

To understand what's happening on the front lines, I sat down with Bernadette Del Chiaro, Executive Director of the California Solar & Storage Association. Bernadette has spent more than two decades advocating for clean energy policy and has become one of the most recognized voices fighting to keep rooftop solar viable in California.

CASE STUDY: FIGHTING FOR FAIR SOLAR POLICY IN CALIFORNIA

Anna: California has long been viewed as the rooftop solar capital of the country—but in recent years, that leadership's been under attack. From where you stand, what's really at stake?

Bernadette: California built the nation's largest rooftop solar market— over 2.2 million installations. But over the past decade, utilities have worked hard to chip away at that success. What's at stake is everything: jobs, energy freedom, and climate progress. Policy made it possible—but policy can also take it away.

Anna: You've been in this fight for over 20 years. What's been the biggest shift?

Bernadette: The moment rooftop solar reached working-class families, the utilities panicked. That's when they started pushing the "cost shift" myth. It was a strategic move, they framed solar as a burden to low-income customers, when in reality it reduces grid strain and brings down costs for everyone. They twisted the equity narrative, even invoking social justice language to justify corporate lobbying efforts.

Anna: And that helped drive the push for NEM 3.0?

Bernadette: Yes. After NEM 2.0, we thought we'd landed in a workable place. But the utilities didn't stop. They hired national PR firms and laid out a coordinated plan to dismantle rooftop solar—while publicly saying they supported it. Groups like NRDC and TURN echoed their talking points, which gave political cover. And with the governor taking money from PG&E during the recall, we lost a critical ally.

Anna: What about the so-called "solar tax"?

Bernadette: That proposal would've charged people for electricity they didn't even use. When that failed, they came back with a "fixed charge" based on income. It made no sense and met massive backlash—people didn't want to give their tax returns to PG&E. In the end, the CPUC passed a $24/month charge. It's less than what utilities wanted, but it still penalizes customers who invest in their own energy future.

Anna: What gives you hope?

Bernadette: The people. Rooftop solar has always polled off the charts— across race, age, and political lines. Our Save California Solar campaign reached over 100 million people. And the lawsuit we filed against NEM 3.0 on June 4, 2025, is currently before the California Supreme Court. We're not backing down.

Anna: What should solar companies be doing right now?

Bernadette: Fund your trade associations. Support advocacy. Engage your customers. The gun lobby turned its customers into its greatest weapon— solar needs to do the same. Every rooftop solar homeowner is a potential advocate. We just haven't organized them at scale. Yet.

If You're Not at the Table, You're on the Menu

Bernadette's story is a powerful reminder: protecting rooftop solar takes more than public support—it requires relentless advocacy, legal action, and unwavering grit. This industry was built by those unapologetically willing to fight for it. Its future? That belongs to the ones still willing to suit up and show up.

And if you think policy can't be exciting? Wait until you hear how a cardboard cutout of the Terminator, a quarter-page ad in the *LA Times*, and one very specific breakfast moment helped launch California's Million Solar Roofs Initiative. Yes, really. The full behind-the-scenes story—complete with political drama, rooftop rebels, and a surprise call from Governor Schwarzenegger—can be found on thesolarcoaster.com/extended-content. Trust me, it's worth the click.

Because it's not just policy that needs a shakeup. The way we sell solar is just as critical. In the next chapter, we'll explore the hybrid sales approach—where urgency meets transparency—and how behavioral science can help you close more deals, build lasting trust, and grow your solar business with integrity.

CHAPTER 4:

THE SWEET SPOT: HYBRID SALES AND THE PSYCHOLOGY OF PERSUASION

This chapter is all about the *why* behind the *buy*. Why do people say yes? What nudges them toward action—or away from it? And how can you structure your solar sales process to align with the way people are already wired to make decisions?

We'll unpack the psychological triggers that influence customer behavior and show how combining urgency with transparency—the hallmark of a hybrid sales approach—can help you close more deals, ethically and consistently. I'll share the exact strategies I use that have helped me maintain a 70% close rate, even in a competitive and skeptical market.

From emotional triggers and social proof to decision framing and temporal discounting, this chapter is packed with tools to help you sell smarter, close stronger, and build lasting trust—well beyond the install. To kick things off, let's start with a quick nod to one of my favorite books on the topic: *Using Behavioral Science in Marketing* by Nancy Harhut. In her book, she dives deep into numerous behaviors, but I feel these 15 are best applied to the solar industry.

Behavioral Science Models at a Glance: The Anna Cliff-Notes Version

1. **Loss Aversion**—People fear losing more than they enjoy gaining. *Solar Sales Application:* Emphasize rising utility costs and how waiting costs them money every month. Use messaging like, "Lock in your energy rate now before prices go up again!"

2. **Endowment Effect**—People overvalue what they already own. *Solar Sales Application:* Frame solar as adding long-term value to their home and energy independence. Once they consider it theirs, they won't want to lose it.

3. **Autonomy Bias**—People prefer making their own decisions. *Solar Sales Application:* Instead of hard-selling, empower homeowners by offering customized plans and letting them feel in control of their choices. Words like "The Choice is Yours" leverage this concept.

4. **Information Gap Theory**—Curiosity drives action when people realize they're missing information. *Solar Sales Application:* Use questions like, "Do you know how much you're overpaying for electricity?" or "The Solar Secret You Missed" to spark interest.

5. **Authority Principle**—People trust experts and certifications. *Solar Sales Application:* Highlight industry certifications, trusted installers, and customer testimonials to establish credibility.

6. **Zeigarnik Effect**—People remember unfinished tasks and are inclined to complete them. *Solar Sales Application:* Follow up consistently with open-ended proposals, teasers, and reminders like, "Still thinking about solar? Let's finish what we started!"

7. **Reciprocity Principle**—People feel obligated to return favors.
   Solar Sales Application: Offer free energy savings reports and bring gifts (or send them in advance) to your solar consultations—this makes customers feel they *owe* you their time or business.

8. **Scarcity Principle**—People desire what's limited.
   Solar Sales Application: Create urgency with limited-time incentives, rebates, or expiring tax credits (e.g., "Only X homeowners in your area qualify for this rebate!" or "Net Metering is filling up fast in your zone; soon you won't get the payback you deserve).

9. **Novelty Theory**—People are drawn to new things.
   Solar Sales Application: Promote cutting-edge solar technology, innovative financing options, or unique system benefits. Think about it, would you open an email with a subject line "What's New in Solar 2025?" Yes, you would, because you're now combining newness with missing gap theory and feel like you need to know what you don't know.

10. **Social Proof**—People follow the actions of others.
    Solar Sales Application: Showcase customer third-party reviews, video testimonials, and a map with neighborhood installations to create trust and credibility.

11. **Labeling Effect**—How people categorize themselves influences their decisions.
    Solar Sales Application: Frame solar buyers as smart, proactive, and financially savvy, reinforcing their decision as part of an elite group of energy-independent homeowners (e.g., "Join thousands of smart homeowners who have taken control of their energy future").

12. **Framing Effect**—The way information is presented (positively or negatively) influences decision-making.

Solar Sales Application: Instead of saying, "Your energy bill is $300/month," frame it as "You're losing $3,600 per year on electricity," making the cost feel more urgent. Highlight long-term gains by framing solar as an investment, not an expense (e.g., "Would you rather pay the utility forever or make your own power?"). Use comparative framing: "This system will cost you less per month than a cup of coffee a day."

13. **Commitment & Consistency Principle**—Once people say YES, they're more likely to stay consistent with that decision.
    Solar Sales Application: Start with Small YES Responses, "Would you like to see how much you could save?"

    a. Use Micro-Commitments — "Should I include battery options in your proposal?"

    b. Reinforce Their Decision — "You wanted energy independence—solar gets you there."

14. **Temporal Discounting**—People naturally undervalue long-term benefits compared to immediate rewards. The further away the payoff, the less motivating it feels—even if it's much bigger. This is hardwired.
    Solar Sales Application: Think about the Solar Assault concept—this is exactly why it works. Telling a homeowner that they'll save $600,000 over 30 years sounds impressive, but it doesn't feel real or personal. Say this instead: "If I handed you a $200 Visa gift card every month, would that change your life?" Most people say yes—because short-term gains are tangible. The value becomes real.

15. **Temporal Landmarks**—Significant moments in time, such as the start of a new year, birthdays, or other meaningful milestones, can serve as powerful catalysts for change.
    Solar Sales Application: Frame the decision to go solar as a timely, transformative milestone. For example, tie the purchase to a temporal landmark with messaging like:

- "Start the New Year with a smart energy move—join thousands of proactive homeowners taking control of their energy future."

- New Home Messaging: "Congratulations on your new home! This isn't just a purchase—it's a fresh start and a milestone in your life. As you turn this exciting page, consider making your new beginning even more impactful by investing in solar energy. Now is the perfect time to join forward-thinking homeowners who are transforming their living spaces into sustainable, energy-efficient havens. Embrace the change, enjoy long-term savings, and make a lasting legacy for you and your family."

To go a little deeper on a few concepts, social proofing is specifically interesting and has the power to skew behavior toward the Magnetic Middle if not managed correctly.

What is the Magnetic Middle?

People tend to gravitate toward perceived norms like metal shavings to a magnet. So essentially, regardless of whether people were previously behaving in a socially desirable or undesirable manner, they tend to adjust their behavior toward what they perceive as normal. In the book *YES!: 50 Scientifically Proven Ways to Be Persuasive* by Noah Goldstein, Steve Martin, and Robert Cialdini, a compelling example related to energy consumption is presented. In this study—conducted by the household energy conservation group—homeowners' energy usage was monitored, and each participant received a report comparing their consumption to that of their neighbors, categorizing them as either "overusers" or "underusers."

The findings were striking: homeowners who were using less power than their neighbors ended up increasing their energy consumption by 8.6%, while overusers reduced theirs by 5.7%. In other words, people adjust their usage to align with what they believe is the norm, regardless of whether that norm is energy efficient[7].

To test this further, scientists modified the report by adding a simple visual cue—a smiley or frown face—to the "report card." When underusers received a report with a smiley face (indicating that their behavior was approved), they maintained their current level of consumption instead of increasing it. Meanwhile, those flagged with a frown continued to reduce their usage.

This phenomenon has broader implications for social proof in areas such as solar energy adoption. When using case studies or video testimonials to promote solar, it's essential that the social proof resonates with the target audience. People are motivated by the "flock effect" only if they feel a similarity with those being showcased. For example, a case study featuring a 65-year-old white male with a pool in his backyard might not effectively persuade a young family in their 30s who have just purchased their first home in a cookie-cutter neighborhood.

Another interesting concept is reciprocity. One study highlighted how waitstaff behavior can influence tips by varying whether they present the check with or without candy. The research showed that when waitstaff gave a single candy with the check, tips increased by 3.3%. When they provided two candies—one per person—the tips jumped by 14.1%. However, an unexpected additional candy raised tips by 23%[8].

How did this work? The waiter first delivered the check with one candy per person. Then, after turning to leave, the waiter abruptly paused, reached into their pocket, and returned with a second candy per person.

---

7 The household energy conservation study can be found in: Shultz, P. W., Nolan, J. M., Cialdini, R. B., Goldstein, N.J., and Griskevicius, V. (2007). The constructive, destructive, and reconstructive power of social norms. *Psychological Science*, 18:429-34.

8 The Tipping Study can be found in: Strohmetz, D. B., Rind, B,. Fisher, R. and Lynn, M (2002). Sweetening the till: the use of candy to increase restaurant tipping. *Journal of Applied Social Psychology*, 32: 300-309.

This extra, unanticipated gesture made customers feel special, as if they were receiving a personal favor rather than standard service.

This approach can backfire if not managed correctly (e.g., if the waiter does this with every table and the customers see it, then they feel deceived), but the key takeaway is that making the customer feel like they're receiving a personal gift has a powerful effect. Another important factor is timing: immediately after receiving a favor, the receiver values it highly, while the giver assigns it less value. Over time, this shifts—the receiver's perceived value decreases while the giver's increases. This principle not only affects business transactions but also personal relationships. The lesson here is to strike while the iron is hot and ask for a referral or follow-up favor sooner rather than later.

In the context of solar energy, this concept applies well once the installation is complete. Delivering a gift basket, sending a live plant in a customized logo-engraved container, or token of appreciation at that moment can be the ideal time to request a review or referral. Moreover, it shouldn't be a one-off gesture. Continually remind and celebrate the customer's excellent decision to go solar—mark the anniversary with a solar-themed birthday card (variable direct mail!) and encourage them to share the love.

While I could go on and on, one key topic that deserves special attention in the solar sales process is offers and incentives. One of the most powerful persuasion tools is the perception of "no strings attached." When homeowners feel there's no pressure or hidden catch, they're far more likely to agree to a consultation. Always lead with clarity, simplicity, and zero-obligation language to reduce resistance and increase engagement.

Another key factor is how we *frame* gifts or rewards. Behavioral science research—like that found in the book *YES!*—shows that when something is given away for free, its perceived value may be reduced. Customers start to wonder, "Why are they giving this to me? Is it not worth much?"

The fix? Attach clear value. Instead of saying, "Get a free Level 2 charger with your solar install," say, "Go solar with an 8 kW+ system and receive our LevelUp bonus: a Level 2 EV charger and professional installation—a $2,500 value." That makes it feel like a reward vs some giveaway.

To take this further, let's bring in Annie Duke's *Thinking in Bets*, a must-read for anyone in sales or leadership. Her frameworks help both customers and companies make smarter decisions by focusing on probability, expected value, and the power of imagining your future self.

This ties directly into temporal discounting—the human tendency to undervalue future rewards compared to immediate outcomes. That's why a 25-year savings estimate often feels abstract, while a $200/month energy bill reduction feels real.

So how do we bridge that gap? Use questions that make the future feel present *and* tap into probability:

- *"What do you think is the likelihood your energy bill will go up this year"* keep going... *"What about next year, or five years from now?"*

- *"If future you could talk to you today, what would they say about locking in a lower energy cost?"*

By asking these questions, you're guiding the customer through a smarter bet by helping them visualize a future they'll thank themselves for.

From Psychology to the Kitchen Table: Applying Behavioral Science to Solar Sales Strategy

Now that we've explored the behavioral science behind how people make decisions, let's bring it back to the kitchen table. Because that's where the deal is won or lost. Let's walk through how you can use these insights in a real conversation to help homeowners connect the dots between their current bill, the rising cost of energy, and what their *future self* will wish they had done.

In addition to all the tips and techniques already discussed, some of the most common mistakes that salespeople make include:

1. **Overselling with Too Much Information**—Bombarding customers with excessive details can overwhelm and deter them.

2. **Dismissing Customers Based on Perceived Solar Savings**—A customer's financial benefit may not be immediately apparent, but that doesn't mean they aren't a good prospect.

I was recently in Maui visiting a client, Cobalt Power Systems, and owner John Paul Berge shared a clip they call "Be Relentless." In the movie *The Boiler Room*, Ben Affleck delivers a powerful lesson: *"Either you're selling them, or they're selling you."* The takeaway? Every interaction is a sale—either you're convincing them of the value of solar, or they're convincing you why they don't need it. Every call, every meeting, is an opportunity to change someone's future.

Leverage The Zeigarnik Effect: They're *Already* Interested

The Zeigarnik Effect tells us that people remember unfinished tasks more than completed ones. If a customer has already taken the step to meet with you, that means the decision is in motion. Don't give them a reason to hit pause. Avoid inserting your own assumptions about what ROI should matter to them. Instead, guide them through a clear, structured conversation that focuses on the tangible benefits of going solar.

While every great closer brings their own style, here are a few of my personal go-to tools: the bill review, understanding incentives, selling the warranty, and highlighting the technology. Each one plays a strategic role in helping the customer feel confident, informed, and ready to move forward.

The Bill Review Strategy: A Game-Changer

One of the most underutilized yet powerful strategies in solar sales is the Bill Review. Here's how to use it effectively:

1. **Show the Bill**

    o   Display a picture of the customer's bill on a screen or place it on the table.

- o Begin with: "*<Customer Name >, I'm sure you're very familiar with this ever-growing bill from your utility company. But have you ever questioned what all these extra fees are?*"
- o Most customers will nod or say "yes."

2. **Break It Down & Simplify the Charges**

- o Review the charges line by line.
- o Use relatable analogies to explain rate structures: "*You know how when you shop at Costco in bulk, you expect a lower rate per item right? Well, the utility company does the exact opposite—the more you use, the more you pay.*"
- o Watch for looks of shock and frustration. Explain demand charges or time-of-use depending on how that said utility operates.

3. **Personalize their Usage**

- o Show their monthly consumption trends and find a relatable pain point:
  "*It looks like your usage spikes in the summer—do you have central air or a mini-split?*" Or "*December usage is much higher, would you happen to be one of those families with award winning holiday lights and decorations?*"
- o Let them share their discomfort with high bills.
- o Double down: "*Have you ever avoided using your AC (heater, lights, etc.) as much as you'd like because you were worried about the bill?*"
- o Most will answer *yes*, giving you the perfect opening to reinforce the problem solar solves.

4. **Highlight Rising Costs & Lack of Control**

o   Show the historical increase in utility rates: *"Did you know that in the past X years, your utility rates have increased by X%? And here's the kicker—utility rates have NEVER gone down."*

o   Ask: *"Have you ever received a discount or rebate just for being a loyal customer?"*

o   The answer will be *NO.*

o   Then transition: *"What if I told you that you could lock in your electricity rate for the next 25–30 years with a low, fixed monthly payment—or even eliminate your bill entirely with a cash purchase? No more surprise rate hikes. No more stress over rising costs."*

By now, the customer is paying attention. They've seen the flaws in their current utility setup and are starting to imagine life with solar. This point is where many reps rush into the proposal—but I've found it's far more powerful to pause and keep the dream alive. Rather than immediately diving into kilowatts and costs, I want to guide them toward envisioning what life could *look and feel like* with energy freedom.

Make it Personal: Future-Proof their Lifestyle

Solar isn't just an economic decision—it's a lifestyle shift. If I get the chance before meeting the homeowner, I'll ask a few of these questions upfront. But let's be real: that's not always possible. Often, you're walking into a home with only a few notes from the setter (if you're lucky), so you've got to rely on your intuition, read the room, and guide the conversation in a way that invites trust.

"Let's make sure you have all the power you need—not just today, but for the future. Tell me about your lifestyle now...and your dream lifestyle. What would it feel like to never worry about an energy bill again?"

The goal isn't to check off every question—it's to get them talking and dreaming. If I already know a key detail, like they're preparing for retirement or just bought a forever home, I won't run through the full list—I'll lean into that milestone and expand the conversation from there.

Here are some of the prompts I use to personalize the conversation:

- Do you have—or plan to get—an EV?

- Are you thinking about a renovation, pool, or hot tub?

- Will your household be changing—kids going to college, a parent moving in?

- Do you ever wish you could just run the AC all day without worrying about the bill?

Tap into Timing and Milestones

People make major life decisions during major life transitions. It's a perfect time to talk solar.

"What's motivating you to explore solar right now?"

- Preparing for retirement?

- Investing in a family legacy?

- Tired of unpredictable utility bills?

- Taking advantage of federal or state incentives before they disappear?

The key is relevance. When solar connects to someone's life, it stops being a "maybe someday" and becomes the obvious next step. And that's exactly how I approach the conversation from here. I'll say something like…

"Now, while a lot of solar consultants skip over the nerdy details—and honestly, that's fine for most people—I want you to know that it all matters to me. When I chose the solar company that I work with, I wasn't just looking at panels and pricing. I needed to know the technology was reliable, the warranty was legit, the value was real, and the company stood behind their work. Because if I'm going to put my name on it—and recommend it to you—it has to be the kind of solution I'd offer to my own family."

Even if I don't ask it directly in the moment, one key factor I always consider is:

"What matters most to this person in the company they choose?"

It's such a powerful framing question that I've built it right into the lead generation flow in my Solar Wizard plugin application for solar companies. Whether they realize it or not, how someone answers that question shapes everything—from how they respond to your proposal to what builds their trust. They boil down to...

- **Warranty**—If peace of mind is what they're after
- **Value**—If ROI drives their decision
- **Technology**—If they want top-tier performance
- **Reputation**—If trust and longevity matter most

You don't want them to ever feel like any of it *doesn't* matter to you—because it should. Warranty, value, technology, and reputation—it all plays a role.

So, while I may not always speak the question out loud, I'm always listening for the answer. And once I know what they care about most, I tailor everything from there.

In the next chapter, we'll talk more about how to set your closers up for success by gathering these insights earlier in the customer journey—so the pitch starts in sync, not from scratch.

But for now, let me show you how I bring this to life next, starting with warranty, technology and then how to sell incentives (there are more than just tax credits people!), set expectations, and build urgency.

How I Sell Warranty

The key factor that made SunPower a no-brainer was its Complete Confidence Warranty—something most competitors didn't offer. This meant that every part of the system—panels, inverter, racking, and monitoring—was covered by one company. While this isn't a standard, there are EPCs like Powur that have maintained this model. Here is how I sell it.

"<Customer Name>, do you have an Apple device?" (Most do.) *"Great! If something happens to your iPhone, you take it to the Apple Store, and if they can't fix it within an hour, they replace it. Right?* (Dramatic Pause) *…Now, try doing that with an Android—you'd have to box it up, mail it to the manufacturer, and wait. Frustrating, right?"*

"The same applies to most solar systems. If an issue arises, you are responsible for contacting the panel, inverter, or monitoring manufacturer—each likely blaming the other. Meanwhile, you're left hiring a contractor out of pocket to remove the panel, package it, and ship it back. And yes, you pay for labor and shipping."

"It's like health insurance—you don't realize what's actually covered until something goes wrong. With Powur's Care 30-year Warranty, you're covered for 30 years. That means, the event that something happens you only need to make one call to handle everything, including labor, shipping, equipment, and repairs. Even if your original installer goes out of business, Powur dispatches a certified technician to diagnose and fix the issue."

So, why did this approach work—even when the system wasn't always the cheapest? Because it connected with how people naturally make decisions. The Apple analogy tapped into familiarity bias, helping customers quickly grasp a complex concept by comparing it to something they already trust. It also encouraged future-self thinking—getting them to imagine how frustrating and costly it would be to deal with repairs down the line. By positioning everything under one brand and one warranty, I reduced choice overload and gave them a clear path forward. In behavioral science terms, I was reducing uncertainty, building trust, and offering the emotional security that comes from knowing they'll be taken care of if something goes wrong.

While this "complete confidence" warranty pitch doesn't work for all solar companies, the takeaway here is this: behavioral science works best when it meets customers where they already are—emotionally, mentally, and practically. If you can eliminate friction, frame the value clearly, and build trust early, you don't have to be the cheapest—you just have to be the easiest to say yes to.

After addressing the financials and giving the customer confidence through a rock-solid warranty, there's one more element that makes or breaks the deal, the technology itself. And here's the truth: most customers don't walk into a solar consultation dreaming about panel wattage, diode configuration, or degradation rates. What they do care about is performance, durability, and whether it's going to work when they need it most.

That's where your job as a solar storyteller comes in. Just like we used behavioral science to frame the warranty through familiarity and future-self thinking, we now turn to visual demonstrations and environmental relevance to sell the tech. Because when people see the difference, they believe the difference.

Selling the Technology the Right Way

As already mentioned, when I started selling solar, it was under the SunPower brand name, which used Maxeon panel technology. One of the most compelling sales tools they provided was called "the cell break kit." It consisted of two paper-thin modules: one representing a conventional panel (Tier 2 or 3) and the other showcasing the Maxeon Tier 1 panel, which was unmatched in performance, backed by a global patent portfolio comprising over 1,650 granted patents and more than 330 pending patent applications[9].

I'll never forget my first sale. I was in-person at a lovely elderly woman's home in Kapolei. I took out the kit and placed one conventional panel into a sealed plastic bag, then did the same with the Maxeon panel. I handed both to the homeowner and asked her to try breaking them in half. The result?

- The conventional panel shattered into pieces. We all gasped.

---

9 https://www.prnewswire.com/news-releases/maxeon-solar-technologies-initi-ates-topcon-patent-infringement-lawsuit-against-rec-solar-holdings-as-302121932.html/

- The Maxeon panel cracked but remained intact, showing only a tiny fracture on the back thanks to their copper-backed panel technology.

This powerful demonstration proved that, even in a catastrophic event, Maxeon panels would continue functioning due to their superior technology. While a crack might reduce efficiency, the panel would still generate power—an undeniable advantage.

This visual demonstration made it effortless for the homeowner to choose quality over a lower-cost, inferior product. "You get what you pay for" couldn't have been truer. In fact, when I later had to switch her to another solution (REC panels), she was furious. The good news? REC also offered a flexible (won't snap under pressure) panel, and after I shared a video demonstration, she was happy to make the switch.

While manufacturers no longer provide physical break kits, solar consultants should still share and manufacture video content and use real-world examples to create the same impact and win trust. It's also essential to tailor the conversation to the customer's environment to prove your industry expertise. Remember, now that technology has reached a parity, the thing they will remember is YOU taking the time to make them feel assured in their decision! Here are some examples…

- Coastal Areas → Salt decay can corrode lower-quality panels. Highlight how your panels offer superior protection.

- Desert Climates → Extreme temperature swings can damage lower-tier panels. Explain why your panels withstand these conditions. Better panels have a lower "temperature coefficient," which means electricity output will degrade slower as heat rises. REC HJT panels have a very low temperature coefficient (this is a good thing).

- Snowy Areas → Ensure that the panels withstand heavy snow loads without cracking. Example: Panels with snow load ratings above 5,400 Pa (like REC or Maxeon) while inferior panels can crack under snow pressure.

- Heavily Shaded Areas → For shaded environments, micro-inverters or optimizers (e.g., Enphase, SolarEdge) prevent system-wide power loss. Half-cut cell panels (REC Alpha, Jinko Tiger) minimize shading impact, while bifacial panels capture light from both sides. Strategic panel placement also helps maximize efficiency.

By educating customers on why your panels are the right fit, you build confidence and stand out from competitors offering lower-wattage, high-failure-rate systems—or those who prioritize sales over customer experience. Even when competitors offer the same equipment, taking the time to explain each customer's unique situation makes you the trusted choice.

Selling the System Price and Tax Credit Like A Pro

By this point in the presentation, you've built trust, uncovered their "why," and positioned yourself as a trusted and savvy consultant.

Could I sell ice to someone in Alaska? Sure. But that's not the goal here.

When I sold under Sunspear Energy, one thing I emphasized—especially when we were doing residential under a commercial-grade operation—was this: the best systems are engineered by the best minds. And not every company has access to that. The same goes for Powur. Their difference in warranty and operations gave me real confidence in the offer.

So, what's your point of leverage? Find it. Use it. That's what builds confidence and separates you from the solar bros.

Let's Talk about System Price

Look, we're all solar pros here. I don't need to walk you through how to compare a before-and-after bill. That part's simple. "Here's your bill today. Here's what it could look like with solar."

Done. What I do want to take a moment to stress—because this is where sales go sideways—is making sure the customer fully understands the tax credit.

If you rush past it, assume they get it, or let them believe it's an automatic refund check from the government—you're setting yourself (and them) up for confusion, complaints, or cancellations. Now while the Big

Beautiful Bill was signed into law as of July 4th, 2025, things change fast, and there are still attractive state tax credits (like here in Hawaii), so let's just briefly cover this for those readers less savvy in the art of the tax credit.

Tax Credit: Explain It Clearly—Every Time

Whether I ask these questions before the appointment (ideal to pick the best financing) or live at the consultation (realistic), the key is clarity. Don't assume anything. Ask the right questions and tailor the explanation accordingly.

Step 1: Are They Working or Retired?

If Retired: *"<Customer Name>, do you have investments, rental income, or retirement withdrawals that require you to pay federal taxes each year?"*

- **YES** → Great. They likely qualify for the tax credit because they have a tax liability.

- **NO** → A cash purchase or standard loan may not make financial sense. Recommend a lease or PPA, which allows them to go solar without needing the tax credit.

> ⚠ **ANNA'S TIP**
>
> Many retirees think they don't qualify—but if they withdraw from a 401(k), IRA, or receive capital gains, they may still owe taxes and can claim the credit. Also, in places like Hawaii, we have a special ruling: instead of claiming the full state tax credit over several years, homeowners can opt to receive 70% of that amount as an upfront cash refund. For example, on a $10,000 credit, you could get $7,000 back in cash—even if you don't owe state taxes. There may be similar loopholes or incentive programs in your area, so it's worth looking into the fine print.

If Still Working: Ask: *"Are you self-employed or a W-2 employee?"*

- **Self-Employed:** Do they pay estimated taxes to the IRS? Almost always YES.

  → Their tax payments will likely qualify them for a refund at filing time.

  → Bonus: They may qualify for business write-offs too.

- **W-2 Employee:** Perfect. Their employer withholds taxes every paycheck.

  → That qualifies them for the tax credit in the form of a refund check when they file.

Pro Tip: Set clear expectations and remind them: the solar tax credit is not a rebate—it's a dollar-for-dollar reduction in what they owe the IRS.

If they've already paid taxes through withholdings and overpaid, they'll see it as a refund. If their tax bill is less than the credit, it rolls over for up to five years.

Build Trust, Reduce Risk!

Have these explanations available in your sales materials, on your website FAQ, and in any disclaimers.

Always include a clear statement like: *"Please consult your tax advisor to confirm your eligibility for nonrefundable solar tax credits."*

The better you are at explaining this, the more trust you build and the fewer *"Why didn't I get my tax refund?"* calls you'll field next year. Lastly, even without the 30% federal ITC, going solar still comes with a host of benefits. From local sales and property tax incentives to increased home value and long-term peace of mind—not to mention the environmental impact—solar continues to be a smart, future-proof investment.

Final Takeaway: Listen First, Sell Second

Success in solar sales starts with human connection—not specs. It's about listening, understanding what matters most, and shaping your offer around their story. Make them feel secure. Make them feel seen. And most of all, make them feel like going solar was the smartest move their future self ever made.

Now that you know how to run the table, it's time to build a team that can keep up. Next up: how to define clear roles for setters and closers—so every lead starts strong, and every deal closes with confidence.

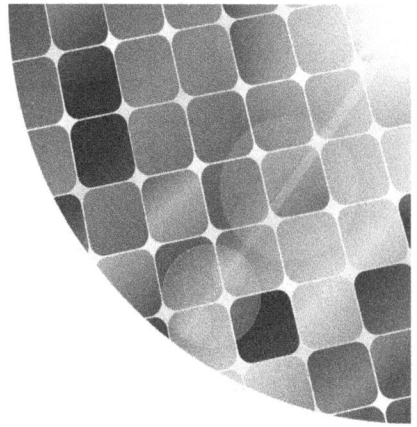

CHAPTER 5:

BUILDING THE SUPER NOVA TEAM

Too many solar companies are bleeding opportunity—not because they lack leads, but because they lack structure. High-intent prospects are handed off to undertrained reps. Outdated scripts are still in play. Deals fall through the cracks because no one's tracking follow-up, objections, or close rates.

And what does leadership do? Yes, they blame the automations. Or worse—they baby the sales team, letting old habits slide because "that's how they've always done it." Instead of holding the process accountable, they shrug it off or keep spending on more leads, hoping volume will fix what discipline won't.

If you're in a leadership role, you have to own your sales machine. Not just set it and forget it—but actively manage it. That means:

- Tracking metrics and conversion stages in your CRM
- Reviewing daily follow-up activity
- Listening to rep calls and objection handling

- Testing scripts and rebuttals
- Coaching in real-time, not quarterly

> ⚠️ **ANNA'S TIP**
>
> Consider charging consultants for leads or appointments.
> They need skin in the game. Why should you carry all the risks?
> Structure success so it's fair for everyone.

Your CRM isn't optional—it's the spine of your business. If your team isn't updating it, they're breaking process and draining your revenue. You can't scale what you can't see. Every lead, call, and quote should be tracked, tagged, and time-stamped. Anything less is just gambling.

There's no magic lead source that can fix a broken follow-up process. The companies that will win the next phase of solar will treat every lead like gold and run a disciplined, transparent sales process from click to close.

It all starts with the handoff—setting the appointment and managing follow-up with precision.

I'm often asked how booking and lead follow-up should be structured. While every team has its own flavor, the foundation is universal: clarity, consistency, CRM discipline, and outreach compliance.

Before You Text, Call, or Email...

Let's keep this short—you can find a more robust breakdown in our resource section (or my other book). Just know this: compliance matters. Whether it's TCPA, A2P 10DLC texting, DNC lists, or email marketing laws, even well-meaning outreach can trigger fines of up to $40,000 per call or $50K+ per email.

Quick hits to stay safe:

- **Texting?** You *must* register for A2P 10DLC. No personal cell phones. No exceptions.

- **Calling?** Know your hours, check DNC lists, and respect opt-outs across *all* channels. Record all calls, inbound and outbound and follow all legal rules for consent notifications; i.e., one party or two party.

- **Emailing?** Follow CAN-SPAM: clear sender info, no shady subject lines, and a real opt-out.

> ⚠️ **ANNA'S TIP**
>
> It might feel easier—or even more personal—to text a lead from your own phone. But don't do it. It's not compliant, it's not professional, and it puts you and your business at risk. Business texting must go through a registered A2P 10DLC platform with proper opt-in and opt-out protocols. One wrong message can trigger fines, shut down your delivery rates— or worse, get your personal number flagged as SPAM. Think about it: do you really want your personal phone number blocked, burned, or blacklisted? Protect your team. Protect your company's reputation. Use the right tools, every time.

Bottom line? It only takes *one* wrong step to jeopardize your entire outreach process. Get flagged as spam, and you risk being blacklisted—or worse, shut down. Plus, holding outdated or unresponsive contacts isn't free—most third-party services charge for every record contacted or, in some cases, held in your CRM. Respect your leads, protect your brand, and move smart.

All right—enough legal talk. Let's get back to building.

Now ask yourself, *"How is your team structured today?"*

Smaller solar companies often rely on multi-hat employees who set appointments, close deals, and manage installs—but that approach doesn't scale. The most efficient, high-performing teams are built on clear role separation, because structure drives results.

In my experience, the strongest solar organizations break their sales process into three core functions: Setters, Closers, and Fulfillment. Let's walk through why this model works—and how to build around it.

Setters and Closers: Why Separation of Roles Works

When it comes to the setter-closer dynamic, there are two schools of thought. Some solar companies believe closers should never call to confirm an appointment, because the moment they do, they start pre-qualifying the lead or projecting doubt. Or worse, they don't call at all out of fear the customer will say the setter was too pushy and cancel the appointment. And while that does happen, what we've found is the real issue goes deeper than the call—it comes down to culture. The challenge isn't just about the closer but about leadership, accountability, and having the right team. At the end of the day, ownership matters most. Someone must make that confirmation call. Fear doesn't win.

I've seen this pattern too many times: assumptions replacing action. A closer hears hesitation, or worse, lets past experiences or ROI bias get in the way, and decides solar just isn't going to work for that homeowner. But that "unqualified" lead? They end up going solar with a competitor who took the time to show up, listen, and do the math.

That's why role clarity matters. Setters set. Closers close. And both take full ownership of their part. The closer needs to do more than just show up—they must be confident enough to make the welcome call, introduce themselves, and reinforce the appointment. Because fear-based decisions—whether it's skipping the call or canceling the sit—don't build pipelines.

And let's be real, you'd rather find out someone's not going to show before you drive 45 minutes across town. But that starts with the setter. They must care enough to book real appointments—not just hit a quota or pass the buck. It's about building a team on both sides that respects the process and understands that every touchpoint, every call, and every confirmation reflects on the company.

Behavioral science tells us people fear making the wrong choice more than they want to make the right one. That's why trust matters—and trust is built through follow-through. If you want to win in this industry, you have to show up—even when it's uncertain. Especially when it's uncertain.

To go deeper, I sat down with two leaders I've had the privilege of working with who've operationalized this mindset. Justin Nielsen of Wolf River Electric and Greg Field of PGT Solar Solutions reveal how role separation, culture, and ownership drive serious revenue.

CASE STUDY: BUILDING SUPER SETTERS: INSIDE THE WOLF RIVER PLAYBOOK

In November 2024, Justin and his team at Wolf River Electric launched an internal transformation that would flip the traditional solar sales model on its head. Based in Minnesota and now serving five states— MN, WI, IA, ND, and SD—Wolf River is rapidly expanding to dominate the Midwest. They handle it all: residential and commercial solar, electrical, and even construction through their parent company, Wolf River Construction, making them an unstoppable force in the region.

As industry uncertainty shook the solar space—policy shifts, rising CAC, dealer chaos—Wolf River leaned in. They didn't flinch. Instead of relying on costly lead vendors or unsustainable sales partnerships, they chose to own every step of the process. What they built was a long-term blueprint for growth, resilience, and control.

Within 12 months, they had created one of the most powerful internal call centers in the industry—generating over 90% of their own leads, training hundreds of new team members each month, and scaling a self-sufficient sales engine that eliminated the need for unstable dealer models or third-party blitz teams. Their approach? Ruthlessly focused on effort over ego, culture over chaos, and consistency over commissions. I sat down with Justin to learn exactly how they did it—and why their model is changing the game.

Anna: Justin, before you built the call center, what was broken about the way solar companies were selling—and what did you see that nobody else was willing to admit?

Justin: The old way—where a rep generates their own lead, runs the pitch, and closes the deal—sounds efficient, but it's not. If you've got someone who's a killer in the seat, why waste their time door-knocking? The best thing you can do for your company—and for them—is to get them in meetings all day. Period.

We knew we had to flip the script. So, we built an internal funnel from scratch. Setters focus on opening the door. Closers focus on converting. And we built a system around that, from recruiting to training to tech. 90% of our sales now come from in-house generated leads. No partners. No fluff. Just performance.

Anna: What's your philosophy behind finding setters who can actually make this thing run?

Justin: Our best setters come from all walks of life: gas station clerks, servers, HR admins, retail workers. What they all have in common is hunger. We give them a clear path: start as a setter, put in the work, and build a life most people only dream about. We rally every morning, live or virtual, and remind each other why we're here. We're creating freedom. Changing lives. Ours and the people we serve.

Not everyone makes it—and that's okay. This isn't a 9-to-5. It's a performance culture. You eat what you hunt. We can teach the systems, the scripts, the tools—but we can't teach hunger.

The ones who show up, stay coachable, and put in the work? They take ownership. And once they taste that kind of freedom, they never go back.

Anna: Let's talk about the people on both ends of the call—your team and your customer base. Most companies assume there's a "type" that fits solar sales and a "type" that buys solar. But you've proven that's not the case. What have you seen when it comes to the range of people succeeding on your team—and who you're actually calling every day?

Justin: What's wild is how wide the range really is—on both sides of the phone. Our setters? Every age, every gender, every background. We've got people in their twenties, and we've got closers in their sixties and seventies crushing it. It doesn't matter what box society put them in. If they've got hustle and can follow a process, they belong here.

And the customers we're calling? Same thing. Most people think solar is just for young homeowners in tech-savvy neighborhoods. Not even close. A huge part of our base is older—retired, fixed income, maybe they've never clicked a digital ad in their life. But they *pick up the phone*. They're curious. And they listen.

That's what makes the call center model so powerful. We're reaching the same audience door knockers are chasing—but we're doing it at scale. While most companies are buying expensive digital leads or relying on third-party providers, we're having real conversations with people who still answer the phone during the day. Boomers. Veterans. Widows. Grandparents. And they're grateful to have someone explain it clearly—without pressure, without a pitch at the door.

Anna: You've got people from all walks of life stepping into this system—and customers who want to talk. But training 100 people a week? That's no joke. What does the machine behind this look like? What's the system that makes all this scalable?

Justin: Yeah, people hear we're training 100 new reps a week and think we're crazy. But that's the system. We built this thing to scale fast, without babysitting. It's structured, it's repeatable, and it's brutal in the best way. The first week is bootcamp. One size fits all. We don't tailor it to personality types or learning styles—we run it like the military. Visual learner, audio learner—it doesn't matter. Get in, gear up, and adapt. If you can't handle the pace or the tech, you're out before you waste your own time. Once they're through training, they're in the seat. Real calls. Real reports. Real accountability. We use GHL for tracking, Slack for communication, and CallTools for dialing. That dialer changed everything. It's the difference between showing up to a gunfight with a musket—or an automatic. You go from making one call at a time to running 10 lines at once. No gaps. No missed chances.

But here's the thing: we still measure people by effort, not just outcomes. The dialer might fire 500 calls, but we're watching who's answering them. Who's logging in. Who's staying consistent. Results come later. Activity tells the truth first.

We don't expect everyone to make it. That's why we're not afraid of churn. It's part of the math. We're looking for the 1%—the ones who rise above. And when we find them, we feed them. Setters become closers. Closers become leaders. And the whole system just keeps getting stronger.

Anna: Why do seasoned closers from dealer networks so often clash with structured teams?

Justin: Because they come in broken—and if you're not careful, they'll break your system, too.

These guys are trained to chase steak. One big deal, one big check, then gone. They're addicted to the kill, not the process. Give them structure and consistency, and they push back. They think they're above it—and worse, they poison your culture.

Here's how I explain it: a dog that gets kibble three times a day is loyal and easy to train. But once he jumps the fence and tastes blood? He's not coming back for kibble. That's your steak-chaser. He doesn't want a system. He wants the high.

That's why we train fresh. No bad habits, just hunger and coachability. We give them a path, and in return, we get loyalty, consistency, and a better customer experience. Everyone wins—the rep, the company, and the homeowner. That's the future.

Anna: Let's talk about what happens after the set—because booking the appointment is just the first step. How do you make sure your closers take full ownership of that handoff, and what kind of results are you seeing from these outbound leads?

Justin: One thing I want to be clear about—the closer has to own the appointment. But before that, the handoff must be clean. The setter doesn't just set and forget it—they're responsible for making sure it was assigned properly, that it landed in the right hands, and that the closer followed up to confirm. It's a team effort up front, but once the appointment's booked and confirmed, it's the closer's job to run with it.

Check the CRM, prep the call, and follow up if needed. That accountability makes all the difference. And we track every step.

Now look—we're not dealing with warm, inbound leads here. These are outbound. People who didn't search for solar. They didn't fill out a form. They just answered their phone. And from that? We're getting a 33% sit rate.

One out of three.

That's huge for outbound. Most companies are used to people who are already halfway sold—form submissions, ads, referrals. Ours? We're starting from zero. Sometimes even negative—skepticism, hesitation, distrust. So, when one out of three still shows up and runs the sit? That tells you our system works. It tells you our team follows through.

Anyone can sell a few jobs when the leads are hot and the market's easy. But if you want to build a real solar company, one that can weather the storm, you need structure. You need people who believe in the process. You need to generate your own demand and train your own army.

That's what we've done. And we're just getting started.

Building a Business Like Wolf River

Building something like Wolf River takes more than drive—it demands clarity, grit, and an unwavering commitment. This kind of company isn't for everyone. But for those who value discipline, teamwork, and long-term vision, it sets a new standard.

Now, before any readers think, *"If they can do it, so can we,"* let's take a dramatic pause.

I've seen firsthand how strategies like cold calling and door knocking can produce wildly different outcomes depending on the market. In more mature regions—like Arizona—we're already witnessing the consequences of oversaturation. Let's be real: there are only so many homeowners. While populations are growing, they're not expanding at the pace some mass-scale marketing groups are dialing. When aged lists get recycled without fresh, one-to-one consent, the system breaks down. People become numb. They stop engaging. They start booking fake appointments or giving false answers—not out of spite (well maybe a little), but mostly from sheer exhaustion.

Success like Wolf River's cannot simply be copied and pasted into any market. It works because the team has intentionally built a sustainable system—one rooted in real conversations, thoughtful follow-up, and a culture of accountability. That doesn't mean they rely solely on outbound strategies. Quite the opposite. A huge part of what makes this model work is a strong, consistent brand presence. I can tell you firsthand that Wolf River invests heavily in visibility—from billboards and traditional TV to radio spots, direct mail and a full-funnel digital marketing engine, they know how to lead the pack.

Now that you've seen how Wolf River built a sales machine from scratch, let's shift gears and meet the hottest closer I know: Greg Field. He closes the gap between interest and action using precision, persuasion, and next-level sales psychology. Here's what it looks like when experience meets execution.

CASE STUDY: ZERO PRESSURE, ALL PRECISION— MEET THE SOLAR INDUSTRY'S QUIET KILLER

Greg first became my client in the summer of 2021, and I was immediately impressed—he was the only SunPower Master Dealer operating under the non-installing dealer model at the time. A true industry trailblazer. Over the past 17 years, Greg has sold solar to more than 5,000 residential customers, earning a reputation as one of the sharpest, most consistent closers in the business.

While others struggled or dropped off during SunPower's collapse, Greg was already ahead of the curve. I watched him pivot fast, partnering with new EPCs, building fresh teams, and bringing in top talent to weather the storm and keep dominating.

But Greg is much more than a closer—he's a leader, builder, and innovator. With roots going back to 2008, he spent over a decade working alongside installing dealers through SunPower, mastering the nuances of high-stakes residential sales long before most reps ever knocked on a door. He's watched the industry evolve—and stayed ahead at every turn.

When lead quality became the biggest challenge, Greg didn't complain—he adapted. In 2019, he launched his own dealership in Arizona and took full control of the process: calling, setting, and closing himself. That first summer, he was writing 2–3 contracts a week and sold over a megawatt solo. No excuses.

Since then, he's built powerful virtual sales teams and trained closers to dominate with presentations that convert. No matter the challenge, Greg doesn't cry uncle. He pivots, refines, and keeps outperforming.

Anna: You built a reputation for dominating virtual sales. How did that transition happen, and why did it work so well?

Greg: It wasn't planned—it was survival. When the pandemic hit, no one wanted reps in their homes. And in Phoenix, driving across town for no-shows was already killing my efficiency. At the same time, you had low interest rates, people sitting at home, and money to spend. It was the perfect storm.

I leaned in hard. Built a clean, high-impact pitch deck in Showpad, tightened my process, and committed to virtual. SunPower gave me lead share priority and eventually made me a Master Dealer. I was running five to seven Zooms a day—no windshield time, no wasted energy. It made me faster, sharper, and way more consistent.

At my peak, I closed 7 megawatts—4 personally, the rest from reps I trained. I didn't have time to babysit. I built the system, led by example, and if someone couldn't keep pace, they fell off. When you strip out the distractions and focus on execution, the results compound fast. I burned out eventually—anyone would at that speed. But it showed me what's possible when you remove the fluff and just sell.

Anna: And now the market has shifted again. What's your focus now?

Greg: This is a time of reinvention. Solar is still a big-ticket sale, but in Phoenix—and really in many markets now—if you don't pair it with a battery, it barely makes a dent in the electric bill anymore. Net metering changes and rate structures have shifted the economics, so customers aren't seeing the quick wins they used to.

Because of that, I went back to my recession-era playbook—focusing on energy efficiency first. Things like attic insulation and duct leakage are huge problems that homeowners often overlook. In fact, most attics aren't properly insulated, and ducts can leak up to 20% of their air. Fixing these issues can drop energy bills immediately, and I can sell that at around $40 a month.

It's a much easier conversation to have right now compared to pushing a $250-a-month solar loan. People get it—it's tangible, it's affordable, and it improves their home's comfort. This approach opens doors and builds trust, which is essential in a tougher market.

Anna: So, you're selling to a different type of customer?

Greg: Exactly. I'm not chasing whales or flashy high-end homes anymore—I'm focused on middle-market homeowners who want to make smart, practical energy decisions. Take, for example, someone with a $3 million home who plans to sell in six months. I'm not going to push solar just because I can make a sale. Instead, I'll be honest and recommend something like adding two batteries and grid-tying the system to maximize value.

I'm not in this for the quick commission—I'm here to provide smart, honest advice that genuinely benefits the homeowner. That's how you build trust and create a long-term brand, which in today's market is more important than ever.

Anna: How do you stay competitive when other reps are selling the same product?

Greg: You don't win by selling the same thing better. You win by creating separation and that starts with your process. When I was pushing REC Alpha, so was everyone else. It turned into a commodity war. Customers would collect three nearly identical quotes, and nobody made money.

So, I pivoted back to Maxeon. Forty-year warranty, real tech advantages, and something most reps couldn't touch. I built my own deck from scratch—86 slides, totally custom to how I sell. I walk the client through the product, the performance, and the real-life value. By the end, they're not just sold on solar—they're sold on *me*.

Anna: So, are you more of a consultant than a traditional closer?

Greg: I'm a hybrid. I educate, but I also guide. I'll ask, *"What do you think the next few sits will tell you that I haven't already covered?"* Or, *"Has anyone actually explained it to you like this before?"* Most of the time, they haven't. I listen. I tell it like it is. And I give people the space to make a decision that makes sense for their situation. If they're close, I'll walk with them across the finish line. Not because I'm trying to close fast—but because I care enough to help them stop shopping and start moving forward.

Anna: And you're expanding into new markets now?

Greg: Yes, but I'm being selective, looking for markets with strong NEM policies, solid utility buyback, and minimal need for batteries. Nevada checks a lot of those boxes. I'm building relationships. Some of my best new partnerships are coming through my manufacturer. They're introducing me to installers and vertical companies that have volume but struggle to close. Their question is always the same: *"Do you know a rep who can actually convert?"* That's where I come in.

I work best with partners who need a trustworthy closer. HVAC companies are a great example—they're already in the home doing service or replacements. They ask the right questions—*"How's your roof? Ever considered solar?"* and when the timing's right, they hand it to me. It's not a cold call. It's a consult. It's warm, fast, and it converts.

Anna: What do you look for in a team—and what does ownership mean to you?

Greg: The biggest mistake most solar companies make is recycling the same "solar bros"—commission chasers who know how to hype a deal but not how to serve the homeowner. I'm not interested in that. I'd rather hire someone with zero solar experience who has ethics, emotional intelligence, and a willingness to learn. I can teach product and process—but I can't teach character. If you're in it just to flash a $10K commission check on Instagram, you're not a fit. This industry doesn't need more hype—it needs people who give a damn.

And once you're on the team, ownership is everything. If a lead hits your calendar, it's yours. You don't blame the setter, the lead source, or the CRM. You call the client, confirm the appointment, do your homework, and show up prepared. I've followed up with leads for six months before getting a response—and that's okay. I'd rather hear a "no" than be ghosted. Trust is built through consistency, honesty, and follow-through—not pressure. The best consultants take full responsibility and show up, even when the lead goes quiet.

Anna: Some reps say they avoid calling leads out of fear they'll cancel. What do you say to that?

Greg: That's fear talking, and fear has no place in sales. If you're afraid to call, you're not ready. I introduce myself, share my 15+ years of experience, and make it clear I'm here to help, not pressure.

If they want to cancel, that's their choice—but most of the time, that call keeps the appointment alive. Avoiding the call only manifests the outcome you fear.

Anna: What do you think the future of the industry looks like for sales guys like yourself?

Greg: It's going to stay messy and that's part of what makes it both a challenge and an excitement. Solar will always face policy shifts, changing incentives, and utility hurdles. I've lived through every so-called "end" over the course of my career, and I used to think every bump in the road was a catastrophe. But now I get it. This industry is a wild ride that demands resilience, grit, and patience. You don't survive by hoping for calm—you survive by embracing the chaos and evolving with it.

Solar isn't going anywhere. Sure, I could fall back on my real estate license like many do—it's a safer bet. But where's the fun in that? This industry matters. It's here to stay, with a lot on the line—our environment, our future, and the lives we change every day.

Real closers care, stay flexible, and embrace the chaos. That's how you win.

"I've been in solar since before tax credits existed—and we still closed deals. If they go away, we'll adapt. Solar isn't just about incentives—it's about control, stability, and long-term value."

– Kelley Barber, Solar Sales & Marketing Leader since 2007

To Wrap Up Setters and Closers

As we've learned, a well-structured setter and closer system is a behavioral blueprint for deeper engagement, higher conversions, and long-term customer loyalty. When aligned with key psychological principles, each stage of the sales funnel becomes a powerful opportunity to guide prospects through decisions that feel intuitive and rewarding.

Setters initiate the relationship, ensuring prospects feel acknowledged and understood. Closers then take the baton, reinforcing trust, overcoming objections, and presenting personalized solutions rooted in the customer's motivations. Throughout the funnel, principles like loss aversion, social proof, the Zeigarnik Effect, and autonomy bias can be strategically applied to reduce friction and drive action.

Here's how behavioral science can power your messaging at key milestones:

- **Unresponsive leads**: Re-engage using scarcity, novelty theory, and the information gap.

- **No-shows or reschedules**: Prompt them with endowment-based reminders, and lost aversion messaging.

- **Proposal sent**: Use social proof and autonomy-driven messages to reinforce trust and momentum.

- **Verbal commitments**: Keep the deal alive with Zeigarnik-style nudges until signatures land.

- **Limbo leads (or not ready for solar)**: These are qualified prospects who aren't quite ready—maybe they're waiting on a utility bill, traveling, or aligning the install with a personal timeline. Respect their request while staying top of mind using temporal landmarks ("after your next bill"), commitment and consistency (referencing previous interest), and identity labeling reinforcement ("for thoughtful planners like you"). Layer in future pacing to help them visualize the benefits ahead and use soft scarcity to maintain relevance without pressure.

Text, email, phone queue, direct mail, and beyond—every channel should work in sync, and your CRM must be the command center, not just a database. From handoff to follow-up, the best teams leave nothing unchecked.

When messaging aligns with behavior—and is delivered with speed-to-lead precision—your CRM transforms from a static system into a true conversion engine, one that anticipates hesitations, celebrates milestones, and builds momentum at every stage.

"The moment a lead clicks 'submit,' a clock starts ticking—not just on your ability to respond, but on their willingness to engage. We call it intent decay. With every passing minute, their focus drifts, distractions pile up, and your window to make a meaningful first impression shrinks fast. Our data shows that if you don't reach out within 5 minutes, your odds of connecting on that first call attempt drop by over 500%. That's not a soft decline—it's a cliff."

– Chaz Tedesco, COO at CallTools

But remember, what separates the pros from the bros are dedication and long-term commitment. You must show up, keep at it (well after the competition stops contacting the same lead), and hold yourself to a higher standard. Don't let fear drive; take the wheel and remember what's at stake here—your future, our world.

Now that your sales team is firing on all cylinders, what happens next is just as critical. The moment a contract is signed isn't the end of the sale—it's the beginning of the customer experience. Whoever takes over at this stage can either reduce cancellations and reinforce confidence or drop the ball and unravel all the trust you've built.

The next section dives into the make-or-break phase of post-contract success—where strategic handoffs, seamless installation coordination, and proactive project management turn customers into promoters who leave 5-star reviews and generate referrals for years to come.

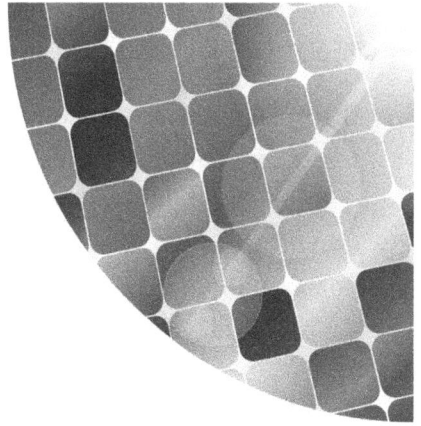

CHAPTER 6:

A SUNSATIONAL INSTALLATION EXPERIENCE

One of the biggest—and most costly—mistakes solar companies make post-sale is failing to assign a clear point-of-contact for the customer. Time and time again, we've seen hundreds of hours wasted because the customer calls their salesperson for an update. Instead of selling, that rep is now logging into the CRM from the road, calling operations, texting installers, and cobbling together a response. It's inefficient. It's frustrating. And worst of all—it's completely avoidable.

Your sales reps should not be your customer service team. Every minute they spend chasing updates is a minute they're not closing new deals. This process drains your pipeline, kills productivity, and erodes customer confidence.

The solution is simple: assign a dedicated project coordinator immediately after contract signing. This person is responsible for all communication, coordination, and customer experience from site survey to permission to operate (PTO). And if your company isn't ready to staff that role full-time? At the very least, implement milestone-based automated messaging that updates the customer at key points in the journey.

Think of it this way: your customer just made a major financial decision—they're investing in energy independence, sustainability, and their home's future. If they don't hear from you for two or three weeks, their trust starts to fade. Silence breeds doubt. Communication builds confidence.

Here's how leading companies handle it:

- A text or email goes out the moment the site survey is scheduled.

- A friendly update is sent when the design is completed and permitting begins.

- A personalized message follows permit approval, prepping the customer for installation.

- After the system is installed, they get a celebratory message and a preview of next steps for permission to operate.

These small, automated touchpoints reduce call volume, prevent frustration, and—most importantly—make customers feel cared for. Your CRM should handle all of this through simple workflows and built-in safeguards that catch communication issues before they lead to cancellations.

The companies that scale stop making sales reps babysit installs—and start empowering customers with clarity. When communication is treated like part of the product, customers trust you more, call less, and refer often.

Post-Installation Wins: How to Turn Projects into Promoters

PTO may feel like the finish line, but it's actually the start of your real growth engine. Too many solar companies treat interconnection as the end, when it's one of the best opportunities to build loyalty, spark referrals, and turn customers into promoters.

Customers won't remember what panels or inverter you installed, but they'll never forget how you made them feel during one of the biggest investments of their lives. How you handle the days surrounding installation and activation can turn one homeowner into a megaphone for your brand.

During Install: The Neighborhood Goldmine

A highly effective yet underutilized strategy is having the energy consultant (EC) show up on install day. Not just to shake hands and bring a small gift (a branded plant, bottle of wine, or thank-you basket), but to turn that installation into a referral machine.

Here's what winning reps do:

- Arrive before or just as the crew starts work

- Greet the homeowner with a thoughtful gift and quick walkthrough

- Let them know *you're their advocate* during the install—any issues, they call you

- Then… go knock on the neighbors' doors

Say something like:

"Hi, I'm with [Company Name]—we're installing solar on [Homeowner's Name]'s home today. Just wanted to give you my card in case the noise or traffic causes any inconvenience. Also, if you've ever thought about solar, I'd be happy to give you a free consultation."

You don't need to pitch—you're just being neighborly. And trust me, people talk. You'll be surprised how many conversations this sparks in the days that follow. Make it memorable by bringing a few company-branded mini waters or a small snack to smooth over any inconvenience their smart neighbor may have caused. Remember the science of reciprocity!

> *"Seeing a SunSolar truck in the driveway—it's our opening move. It tells the whole neighborhood this install was done right, by one company, start to finish. Then we knock every door on the block and turn that trust into leads."*
>
> –Michael O'Donnell, SunSolar Solutions

Flip the Switch: Turning PTO into a Party

In Chapter 1, I mentioned the "Flip the Switch" Solarbration—and it's worth repeating here. If the homeowner is open to it, this is an amazing moment to:

- Host a small gathering (just the customer and a few neighbors)
- Bring snacks, lemonade, or simple giveaways
- Take a short video of the moment the system is turned on (yes, you can fake it)
- Share that video (with their permission) in your marketing or social channels

Want to go even bigger? Send a postcard or flyer to the block inviting them to a neighborhood "solar social." It builds trust, encourages questions, and positions your customer as a local success story.

Bonus: You can track attendees and offer the homeowner a referral reward if anyone they invite signs up later. You've just turned a PTO moment into a lead funnel. What could make this even yummier? Your company's branded mobile showroom — an Ice Cream Truck! :0) Have fun. It's the best way to attract authentic opportunities.

Post-PTO Follow-Up: Small Effort, Big Impact

Once the system is live, don't let the energy fade. Even if you can't do the full Solarbration, the rep should still call to:

- Congratulate the customer
- Ask for a review while the experience is still fresh, and we know they're happy
- Remind them of your referral program
- Send a handwritten thank-you note or gift (yes, you can automate this with variable printing; we do it all the time for clients, and it's just as effective because we know they are sent every time, not just some of the time). Believe it or not, I have client data to support that a simple "thank you for meeting with me" postcard can increase close rates by 5-15% so think about what a "thank you for picking us" can do for your referrals!

These little touches separate transactional companies from trusted and cherished brands.

The 30-Day Check-In: Your Reputation Safety Net

Roughly 30 days after PTO, the customer will likely receive their first utility bill. This is where questions and confusion often arise:

- "Why is my bill still showing charges?"
- "How do I track how much energy I'm producing?"
- "What's that new line item from the utility?"

A call from your project coordinator or customer success manager at this exact moment can catch confusion before it turns into frustration. It's also a prime opportunity to:

- Confirm everything is working properly
- Educate the customer on how to read their bill
- Ask for feedback (short surveys are ideal here, either through the phone, text, or email) and record them in your CRM.

> ⚠️ **ANNA'S TIP**
>
> If the install was rough or communication fell short, don't ask for a review—fix the experience first. Route unhappy customers to a senior team member who can respond with empathy and authority. You might turn a critic into your biggest promoter. We use a 5-question survey: scores of 4–5 trigger a review request; scores of 1–3 flag the account for follow-up by management.

One-Year Anniversary Touchpoint: Solarbrate Your Success

Twelve months after install is a powerful and underutilized milestone. A quick email or mailer can recap:

- Estimated savings on electricity that year
- Environmental impact (CO_2 offset, trees planted, etc.)
- A thank-you message for being part of the solar movement

This is the perfect time to:

- Reintroduce the referral program
- Offer new services or remind them of what they might not have taken advantage of prior—EV level 2 charger, maintenance/panel cleaning package, smart panel, or even storage add-ons. Just because they didn't buy it on the first round, doesn't mean they don't wish they did (think about the Ambrose case study and Pat's example). This happens often, in fact I personally sold another Tesla Powerwall 2 to a customer just six months after install when they realized that my initial recommendation for three Powerwalls was the right number based on their usage.
- Share any updates or promotions.

It's also the perfect moment to reinforce pride. Help your customer feel great about their decision—again. That feel-good energy fuels referrals and boosts the chance they'll share your name organically. Tapping into the power of happy customers is more important than ever. Go the extra mile: send something memorable, like a desk plant or moss plaque engraved with your logo. A branded bumper sticker or a quality hat goes a long way, too. After a year of savings, they'll wear it proudly—if you sold it right.

Remember the 80/20 rule: 80% of your business will come from 20% of your customers. Make those 20% feel seen. Here in Hawai'i, we treat everyone like 'ohana—family. That's why today, 100% of my leads come from referrals. I love to "talk story" with my clients—and yes, they really do become 'ohana.

Automation with Intelligence: Protect Your Brand

Yes, CRM automation is essential. It saves time and ensures consistency. But automation without strategy is risky.

Here's how to do it right:

- **Trigger smart automations** based on real milestones (PTO, first bill received, one-year mark)

- **Build in safeguards** to suppress marketing to customers who give low feedback scores

- **Flag negative survey responses** for human review and intervention—*before* they leave a public review

- **Use tagging or lead scoring** to identify promoters (ideal referral asks) and detractors (needs attention)

Automation should amplify great experiences—not multiply bad ones.

Where Install Ends, Leadership Begins

A well-executed, transparent installation process builds systems and trust. And trust turns into reviews, referrals, and long-term brand loyalty. But your job doesn't end when the panels go up. As a business owner, you must anticipate what matters most post installation—especially at the local level. Take True-Ups, for example: in some Net Energy Metering (NEM) markets, this annual billing reconciliation can surprise customers if they don't fully understand how their solar production aligns with utility billing cycles. Depending on when they installed, they might owe money or lose credits if they're not informed, and typically there is only one chance to change an anniversary date.

While True-Ups don't apply everywhere, the principle does: you need to proactively build region-specific knowledge into your follow-up process. That could mean automated tax reminders, local incentive or program updates, or even billing guidance tailored to utility rate changes.

Be proactive. Be local. Be the leader who adds value. Now that's something to Solarbrate!

Beyond the Install: Turning Service into Strategy

With millions of systems now online nationwide—and many "orphan" solar homeowners left without service—the demand for operations and maintenance (O&M) is skyrocketing—and the smartest teams are leaning in.

O&M goes far beyond just fixing things. It creates recurring revenue, extends customer lifetime value, and transforms trust into long-term loyalty. From battery upgrades and critter guards to storm alerts and panel cleanings (including drone-assisted options), there's a full menu of services solar companies can offer. With the right tech stack, much of it can be automated, bundled, and scaled.

For commercial clients, proactive maintenance is even more critical. Missed system faults can lead to six-figure losses—we've seen it happen. That's why leading companies are doubling down on real-time monitoring, performance tracking, and predictive maintenance tools that prevent small issues from becoming major problems.

"Trust doesn't end at PTO—it begins there. The best brands turn maintenance into momentum."

– Brian Kelley, Sea Bright Solar

Some companies have launched dedicated service arms to handle re-installs, EV charger and storage add-ons, drone-enabled panel cleaning, and warranty claims. The result? Fewer support tickets, happier customers, and a business model that goes beyond one-time installs.

Truth is, if you're not thinking about post-install support, your competitors are. It might not seem like a big moneymaker, but it's steady, scalable revenue. I have clients pulling in millions a year—just from maintenance packages and follow-up services. And those numbers? They're only going one way—up, up, up.

Beyond O&M: Adding New Revenue Streams with Commercial EV Charging

O&M is just one piece of the post-installation puzzle. For companies ready to go further, expanding into Commercial EV Charging as a Service (CaaS) offers a powerful new revenue stream.

Instead of selling equipment outright, CaaS allows your company to own, operate, and manage EV chargers for businesses under a subscription model. It's a win-win: businesses get turnkey infrastructure without the upfront cost, and you gain long-term recurring revenue from service agreements and energy sales.

Whether bundled with solar or offered as a standalone service, commercial EV charging enhances your value proposition, attracts new clients, and future-proofs your business for the electrified economy.

By adding CaaS to your offerings, you're leading a transformation.

> *"When you stop thinking like a solar company and start thinking like an energy company, that's when real scale happens."*
>
> – Vladimir Marchenko, Wolf River Electric

And that's exactly what the next chapter is all about: scaling with intention. Building on this momentum, we're diving into what it really looks like to grow—strategically and sustainably. From vertical integration to entirely new revenue streams, you'll meet the innovators reimagining what a solar company can be. Grab your popcorn—this section is juicy.

CHAPTER 7:

SCALING YOUR BUSINESS: TALES FROM THE STREETS

Now that you're building your business the right way, it's time to focus on scaling strategically. In this chapter, we'll dive into a series of case studies from industry leaders who have successfully expanded into new verticals to adapt to the evolving solar landscape.

But before we get into future-focused growth strategies, I want to start with some hard-earned lessons from my home state of Hawaii. Too often, I hear companies throwing in the towel when net metering policies change—as if it signals the end of the industry. Let me be clear: Hawaii ended NEM in 2015, and the solar market here is *still thriving*. Those who adapt, survive. Those who innovate, thrive. And those who complain? Well... they don't last long.

You have everything you need to grow into the future, you just need to learn from the right people. That's why we're starting this section with a case study featuring Gabriel Chong, Chief Engineer of Sunspear Energy. Gabriel wasn't just the first licensed SunPower engineer in Hawaii—he also installed both of my home solar systems: the first, an early investment by my father before I was even in the industry, and the second, while I was actively working for Sunspear Energy. More than that, Gabriel was the person who taught me how to sell solar. He's a true master of his craft, and his insights will help you see what's possible when you evolve beyond the basics.

CASE STUDY: THE END OF NEM – PARADISE LOST & REGAINED

Anna: What was it like before the end of NEM in Hawaii?

Gabriel: It was the Wild West—but in the best way possible. Solar in Hawaii was a no-brainer. Permits flew through, no one needed batteries, and interconnection was practically automatic. The economics? Unmatched. You didn't have to sell solar—you just had to show up. It was a land rush. Everyone wanted in, and for good reason. We were living in the golden age of PV, when the sun shone bright on every rooftop and the grid was still wide open. Then… the moratorium hit. And everything changed.

Anna: So, the moratorium was a turning point. What happened, and how did the industry react?

Gabriel: It was like the music stopped mid-song. Hawaiian Electric Company (HECO) slammed the brakes to prevent grid instability, and while their reasoning was technically sound—too many outdated, "dumb" inverters were threatening system reliability—the timing was brutal. Contractors were blindsided. Projects froze. Sales pipelines dried up overnight.

At the time, I was already at Johnson Controls, past my Sunetric chapter. For us, it wasn't as disruptive—our commercial projects had already been approved or were tied into state and federal interconnection processes.

But for residential installers, it was a gut punch. If you had a backlog of sales and hadn't submitted permits, those projects were dead in the water. Suddenly, everything was being judged against HECO's new Locational Value Map (LVM), which determined whether your project could even connect to the grid.

It took six to twelve months for the utility to implement smarter inverter requirements and roll out the consumer Customer Grid-Supply (CGS) program. But at just $0.15 per kWh, CGS wasn't economically viable. The market collapsed for anyone relying on exports.

That's when energy storage went from being a luxury to a necessity. You couldn't just sell PV anymore. Batteries became the only way to make projects pencil out. And a lot of companies couldn't pivot fast enough.

We watched contractors drop like flies. Some gave up entirely; others rebranded as HVAC, electrical, or smart home companies just to stay alive. It was an identity crisis for the whole industry. But it also forged the most resilient players—the ones who could adapt, think ahead, and survive the storm.

Anna: How did that period shape today's market?

Gabriel: It weeded out the weak. The strongest contractors are still standing because they think long-term. Solar is an infinite game—if you can't adapt, someone else will eat your lunch. Now we're seeing stability, but there's always the looming possibility of change. The successful ones are already planning five to ten years ahead.

Anna: With net metering policies changing rapidly across the mainland, what's your take? What should contractors be learning from Hawaii's journey?

Gabriel: Honestly? If you're still building your business around PV-only systems, you're living in the past. Hawaii already went through the crash course in what happens when net metering ends—and we've come out the other side smarter, leaner, and better equipped.

We learned the hard way that resilience sells. When PV alone stopped making financial sense, the companies that could communicate the value of backup power, energy arbitrage, and peace of mind didn't just survive—they grew.

Mainland contractors should take note: the shift is happening faster than you think. Customers want control, not just savings. And if you're not offering that, someone else will. Hawaii's journey is a blueprint. Ignore it at your own risk.

Anna: How should contractors be thinking about financing models like leasing, especially as costs rise and markets shift?

Gabriel: Leasing can be a useful tool—but only if it's grounded in the reality of your market. In high-cost areas—whether it's Hawaii or California—a lot of national companies come in with unrealistic expectations. They assume they can fund 50 systems with $1 million, then realize that with local labor, storage requirements, and material costs, they're barely covering 20.

To spread risk, they try to sign up as many customers as fast as possible, hoping volume will compensate for razor-thin margins. But that's a dangerous strategy. If you're chasing high margins on low volume, you're setting yourself up to fail. Contracting is a volume game—and you need consistency, not just short-term wins.

Equipment quality is another factor that often gets overlooked in lease portfolios. Some companies push unproven products just to keep costs down. I've seen firsthand what happens when that backfires. Take SunPower's SunVault, for example—it was one of the worst batteries ever created. It damaged customer trust and the brand's reputation, and ironically, it only made Tesla's reliability stand out more.

> *"SunPower had the strongest brand in solar and followed it up with the most unreliable battery in the market."*

Tesla Direct and other near-zero-margin models may seem like a competitive threat at first, but they often rely on bait-and-switch pricing or upsells.

In the end, customers pay about the same—just with less clarity. That kind of strategy erodes trust in the long run.

And for those worried about incentives drying up: yes, they change, but the value proposition of solar goes far beyond bill savings. Homeowners reinvest that money into roofs, windows, EVs—you name it. Contractors who focus only on the numbers miss the bigger picture. Those who understand how to deliver true value—energy independence, resilience, and transparency—will be the ones still standing five years from now.

Anna: So, what should contractors and customers really be paying attention to now?

Gabriel: Misunderstanding and misrepresentation. That's the biggest threat to the solar industry today. Policies will always shift. Programs will come and go. But it's the bad sales practices that leave the deepest scars. The rise of the "solar bros"—slick talkers in polos pushing flashy deals with zero transparency– has been one of the most damaging trends we've seen. These aren't energy advisors. They're salespeople with scripts. They get customers focused on the monthly payment and bury the true cost in fine print. Commissions get padded, accountability disappears, and when something goes wrong—guess who's not answering the phone?

It's no different from the worst kind of car sales tactics: *"What kind of monthly payment are you looking for?"* That mindset doesn't build energy independence, it builds regret. Especially with leases, where the contractor has little incentive to service the system quickly. As long as it's producing at 80%, they've met their obligation. But that means 20% of your system could be down for months while no one lifts a finger. That's unacceptable. When someone buys with cash or a loan, the contractor has skin in the game. There's a vested interest in keeping that system running at full capacity, because your reputation and referrals are on the line.

If there's one lesson mainland markets should take from Hawaii, it's this: the sales game has to grow up. This industry needs to shift from hype to honesty. Sell on truth. Sell on trust. And that's how we fulfill the real promise of clean energy.

Knowing When to Switch Gears

Gabriel's story is revealing because what happened in Hawaii will, in some form or another, happen elsewhere. Market shifts are inevitable. The real question is: will you recognize the signs in time to adapt?

Knowing when to pivot is one of the most important skills a solar business can develop. And it doesn't always take a full-blown policy crisis to trigger that need—sometimes, the writing is on the wall long before the rules change. Maybe margins are tightening. Maybe customers are asking sharper questions. Maybe your sales team is burning out chasing deals that no longer pencil.

That's precisely where many of the companies I've worked with found themselves. They started with deep roots in residential solar or early-stage clean tech but recognized the signals of an evolving industry. Instead of waiting for the pipeline to stall, they adapted—pivoting into higher-margin, future-focused verticals. What do they all have in common? They navigated change and kept growing.

Now let's look at how one leader transitioned from residential sales to utility-scale solar, focusing on land acquisition and agricultural partnerships. Then we'll explore clean energy innovation across critical infrastructure—marine, highways, airports—with a leader redefining what deployment looks like. You'll also meet a commercial solar expert who evolved from the EV space, leaning into product innovation and strategic partnerships to fuel his next chapter.

Let's start with Paul Sullivan, who was responsible for me being invited into the SunPower preferred network back in 2017. Thanks, Paul!

CASE STUDY: FROM RESIDENTIAL SALES TO UTILITY-SCALE IMPACT

After nearly two decades in solar, Paul Sullivan has seen the industry from all sides—sales, partnerships, land development, and beyond. He began his journey in 2006 with one of the first SunPower dealers, later joining the company directly and helping shape its evolving dealer network. When SunPower's strategy shifted and the market began to fracture, Paul pivoted—partnering with ESA Solar an Orlando, Florida-based company to launch their California non-installing dealership.

That move positioned him perfectly for the next phase: stepping out of residential and into utility-scale and community solar development. Today, Paul is a top land acquisition manager for ESA Solar, with a focus on agricultural communities across the country. From rooftop savings to multi-generational land leases, his work continues to center on relationships, trust, and building long-term value for families and communities alike.

Anna: After so many years in residential sales, what drew you to land acquisition and utility-scale development—and what made it feel like the right next chapter?

Paul: After years in residential solar, it felt like coming full circle—but with even more meaning.

I'm still sitting at kitchen tables, but now I'm not selling a system—I'm offering a partnership. A 40-year land lease that can change the financial trajectory of a family for generations. It's one of the most rewarding chapters of my career. We've gone from helping individual homeowners save on their monthly bills to helping entire communities build long-term economic stability. Community solar, utility-scale development, energy storage—it's all connected. And at the heart of it, it still comes down to trust, relationships, and impact.

Anna: What kind of impact are you seeing for these landowners?

Paul: I see it as life changing. Many of these families have been farming the same land for generations, barely getting by. In a good year, they might make $1,500 to $1,800 per acre—but after machinery, fertilizer, and other costs, they're lucky to pocket $200 or $300. It's a volatile livelihood. Now picture this: we come in and offer anywhere from $700 to $1,400 per acre depending on the state and land value, with an average of around $1,200—guaranteed—with annual increases built in, either through a

2% escalator or CPI indexing. And it's locked in for 40 years. That kind of consistent, reliable income? It's transformational.

There's one family in Indiana I'll never forget—the parents and their son were all driving school buses just to pay for health insurance and to make ends meet. Today, thanks to a solar lease, they're earning a six-figure income by walking to the mailbox. They kept their land. They stayed in their community. And they secured a future for their kids and grandkids. That's the kind of impact that keeps me going every day.

Anna: And the community impact?

Paul: It's just as powerful. Agricultural land typically brings in very little property tax—but once we develop it for solar, that same land can generate over a million dollars a year in new revenue for the county. That kind of funding doesn't just sit in a budget—it shows up as a new firefighter, a staffed ambulance, a teacher in the classroom, or a community program that would've otherwise been out of reach.

And we don't stop there. We invest back into the communities—supporting local chambers, funding scholarships, even restoring a small agricultural museum in Arkansas. These aren't just solar projects. They're economic engines. They're stories of resilience and progress. They're about people, legacy, and futures that are now possible.

Anna: What about resistance—how do you handle concerns about taking over farmland?

Paul: That's the most common objection we hear. I did a deep dive into this back in my home state of California, and what I found really changed the conversation. Most of the corn being grown isn't for human consumption—it's for ethanol. And soybeans? They're going to biodiesel. So, I tell landowners: you're already in the energy business—you just haven't been getting paid like it.

When you compare it side by side, solar can generate up to 800 times more energy per acre than an acre of corn being grown for ethanol. And instead of dealing with unpredictable markets, rising input costs, and climate swings, you're getting stable, long-term income. It's not about taking land away from food—it's about rethinking how we use land to support both our economy and our energy future.

Anna: You've talked a lot about utility-scale and land development, but I know community solar has a special place in your heart. What drew you to that model?

Paul: Community solar is one of the most inclusive models in the entire industry—and I love it for that reason. I actually signed the very first community solar lease in California for ESA. The legislation was in place, but the rules hadn't even been written yet. We were ahead of the curve. What makes it so powerful is the accessibility. You don't need to own a home. You can be a renter, a church, a school, a nonprofit—anyone can subscribe and see 10–20% savings on their electric bill. It's structured like a co-op, and in most states, your subscription is portable. So, if you move across town, you can take it with you.

It opens the door for low- and middle-income households to participate in clean energy—people who've traditionally been left out of the solar conversation. And on the developer side, it's a different kind of satisfaction. You're expanding equity and giving people energy freedom they didn't have before.

Anna: Any final thoughts as we close?

Paul: Just this—I feel lucky to be in a part of the industry where the work truly matters. We're not just building solar projects. We're creating generational income for landowners, funding local infrastructure, and delivering clean energy when the grid needs it most. Utility-scale solar with storage is the fastest, most affordable solution to meet rising demand. And despite all the ups and downs, this chapter of my career has been the most fulfilling yet. We're only getting started—and the impact ahead is going to be massive.

Final Thoughts

Paul's journey is proof that solar is no longer just about panels on roofs—it's about reimagining how energy intersects with land, legacy, and local economies. From farmland leases that reshape family futures to community solar programs that expand access and resilience, Paul has shown how thinking beyond residential can unlock deeper impact and longer-term value. Which brings us to the next shift—innovation on the ground. Literally.

As the solar industry pushes beyond rooftops, standing out takes more than panels and permits—it takes vision. Anthony Baro is a true industry pioneer and reimagining what clean energy deployment can look like, from ports and highways to airports.

CASE STUDY: FROM FLOATING MICROGRIDS TO SMART HIGHWAYS AND AIRPORTS, ONE VISIONARY IS REWIRING AMERICA'S ENERGY FUTURE

Before most people had even heard the phrase "electrification of transportation," Anthony Baro was already building it.

While the solar industry sprinted to put panels on rooftops and auto manufacturers raced to electrify their fleets, Anthony quietly tackled the pieces no one else was talking about—the overlooked infrastructure required to meet our nation's growing appetite for sustainable power.

I first met Anthony in 2021 during a brief call about his expiring SunPower DPF credits. The call lasted five minutes. The impact of that conversation? It hasn't stopped.

At the time, he was already well into transforming E2SOL, his renewable energy development firm, into a force driving the convergence of solar, energy storage, mobility, and intelligent infrastructure. But his vision began much earlier—with boats.

In 2016, Anthony co-founded PowerDocks, a company designed to bring renewable energy, informatics, and sustainability to aquatic environments—something almost no one was thinking about at the time. He saw the future of boating not as a luxury market but as a critical and underserved sector in the clean energy transition. When he looked at a marina, he saw potential charging stations, microgrids, and floating platforms generating and managing their own power.

This wasn't theory. PowerDocks launched the first-of-its-kind floating microgrid capable of powering electric boats and marine operations off-grid, using solar panels, energy storage, and smart data. By 2018, the company had already received the National Marine Manufacturers Association Innovation of the Year Award and multiple other honors. In 2021, E2SOL acquired all outstanding shares of PowerDocks, rebranding its solutions under the name POWER+DOCKS and integrating it into a larger electrification platform.

And while that level of vision might have been enough innovation for an entire career, for Anthony, it was just the beginning. Since then, he's continued to push the boundaries of what energy infrastructure can be—pioneering patent-pending technology that transforms passive spaces like highway medians into active, distributed energy networks. Now, with one eye on the road and the other on the sky, Anthony is helping shape the next evolution of electrification. From fast-charging corridors to energy-resilient airports preparing for electric air taxis and commuter flights, his work is already laying the groundwork for a future where renewable energy and smart mobility are seamlessly integrated.

Anna: Anthony, most people wouldn't have thought to start their electrification journey with boats. Why marine infrastructure?

Anthony: No one was thinking about how boats would charge or how marinas would adapt. I saw a massive gap, and an opportunity. Boats were getting cleaner, but the infrastructure was still stuck in the diesel age. That's why we created PowerDocks. We designed floating, solar-powered microgrids that could generate and store energy off-grid, and we brought smart tech into marinas before anyone else did. We built them to be modular, mobile, and scalable so they could work in everything from remote mooring fields to busy urban marinas.

Anna: Did you expect it to take off the way it did?

Anthony: We knew it was the right idea, but the recognition surprised us. Winning the Innovation of the Year award from the National Marine

Manufacturers Association in 2018 validated the market need. But more importantly, it showed that people were ready to think differently about how infrastructure could evolve. That gave us the momentum to keep expanding.

Anna: And that momentum carried over into your work on land—specifically highways. Can you tell us about your Smart Highway Initiative?

Anthony: Absolutely. Highways are probably the most underutilized infrastructure in America. We have all this real estate—concrete medians—that just sits there. We asked, why not turn those into energy-generating assets? So, we designed a solar beam system that installs directly into the median, complete with battery storage and microinverters. It generates power and supports EV fast charging at rest stops and exits. We've filed patents and partnered with companies like Yotta Energy to integrate their storage technology directly into our platform.

Anna: That's a big shift from marine to roadside. What makes your approach to highway electrification unique?

Anthony: We don't treat highways like a retrofit. We design with energy in mind from the start. This isn't just about throwing up a few chargers at rest stops—it's about creating a distributed, scalable energy network that turns the highway itself into part of the grid. What most people don't realize is that in the U.S., our existing charging infrastructure just isn't built for long-distance travel. You can't drive cross-country confidently because there's no guarantee of fast, accessible charging along the way.

Meanwhile, Europe is already solving this. Countries like Germany are integrating EV fast-charging into their Autobahn system—dedicated zones with high-speed chargers powered by renewables. That's the standard we need to match. Our Smart Highway Initiative is designed to do just that—using highway medians as energy assets to power fast-charging infrastructure where it's needed. It's modular, intelligent, and built to support the real-world demands of electrified mobility in America.

Anna: You're also working on airport electrification. What are you seeing in that space?

Anthony: Airports are about to get overwhelmed. Between electric ground service vehicles, private EVs, commercial aircraft, and the coming wave of eVTOL passenger drones, the power demand at these hubs is about to skyrocket—and most of them aren't ready. The typical airport infrastructure is reactive. We're taking a proactive approach by designing integrated systems that combine solar, battery storage, and smart grid technology to make airports energy self-sufficient.

One of the most exciting areas we're pioneering is wireless charging—specifically, a Bluetooth-based energy transfer system for electric aircraft. Think about it: traditional corded chargers are bulky, limit mobility, and waste energy through resistance, especially at scale. Our solution eliminates the need for physical cables. It wirelessly transfers power from stationary commercial storage solutions to aircraft systems with greater efficiency and flexibility. That's a game-changer for charging electric planes, autonomous passenger drones, and airport support vehicles.

From a consumer standpoint, we're on the edge of a huge shift in short-range commuter travel. Those small "puddle jumper" flights—think 30 to 100 miles between regional airports—are being replaced by 100% electric passenger drones and eVTOL aircraft. They're quieter, cleaner, and drastically reduce the carbon footprint of regional aviation. But to make that reality scalable, we need infrastructure that's just as forward-thinking as the aircraft. That's what we're building.

Anna: What connects all of these projects—marine, highways, and airports? Is there a common thread?

Anthony: Integration. We're connecting power generation, storage, and intelligent controls into one seamless ecosystem. Whether it's a dock, a highway, or a runway, the mission is the same: deliver clean, reliable power exactly where it's needed. The age of single-purpose infrastructure is over. We're creating platforms that evolve, scale, and serve multiple functions in real time.

Anna: What does the future of electrification look like from where you stand?

Anthony: It's everywhere. It's embedded. You won't even notice it—it'll be part of your everyday life. Streets will power your cars. Rooftops will fuel your flights. Airports will act like microgrids. The infrastructure won't just support mobility—it *will be* the mobility. That's the shift we're engineering.

Wrapping it Up

Anthony's work through E2SOL is a powerful reminder that true innovation shapes trends. Whether it's charging your EV during a highway pit stop, flying on a zero-emission aircraft, or docking an electric boat, the systems being built today will define how we live and move tomorrow. He's a true energy hero, building the connective tissue of a clean energy future—quietly, intelligently, and relentlessly.

But even the boldest leaders face friction. Because being first—while visionary—often means running ahead of the market. Up next, we'll look at what happens when the timing isn't quite right, and how one founder turned early insights into a diversified, future-proof solar business.

CASE STUDY: KNOWING WHEN TO PIVOT: LESSONS FROM THE EDGE OF INNOVATION

At a time when the solar industry was still focused on rooftop arrays and net metering battles, Jim Meringer was looking ahead to a future where every home would need to power an EV, where battery storage would be the norm, and where electrification wouldn't just be a feature—it would be the expectation.

When I first met Jim in late 2021, he was already deep into the convergence of solar and EV charging, designing systems that could accommodate the increased electrical demand most homeowners hadn't yet anticipated.

But here's the thing: sometimes being early means being *too* early.

Jim's instinct was right, but consumer adoption didn't move at the pace he predicted. While he was preparing customers for bi-directional charging and vehicle-to-home integration, many were still wrapping their heads around their first EV—and balking at the idea of bundling solar, storage, and advanced energy systems into one massive leap. Instead of jumping in all at once, customers were taking the transition step by step.

Rather than doubling down on a model the market wasn't ready for, Jim adapted. He shifted his focus toward scalable commercial solar projects, leaned into utility-scale work, and began developing product innovations that solved pain points across multiple market segments.

Anna: Jim, you were early to see the link between solar and EV adoption. Where do you think things stand now?

Jim: EV adoption is growing steadily, despite what the headlines suggest. Battery prices have dropped dramatically, from over $1,000 per kilowatt just a few years ago to closer to $250 today. That's making EVs more accessible, and as more people start charging at home, the connection to solar becomes obvious. Energy independence extends far beyond the rooftop, it's about how you power your home, your car, and your life.

Anna: But the market wasn't quite ready for that full leap when you started, right?

Jim: Exactly. I expected customers to jump in all at once—EV, solar, battery, the whole ecosystem. But what I found was that people preferred a phased approach. They'd buy the EV, wait and see how it affected their electric bill, and then consider solar. It wasn't hesitation—it was bandwidth. That's when I realized we needed to pivot—meet the market where it is, not where we think it should be.

So, we shifted. We leaned into commercial solar, where the economics are clearer and decisions are often made with a longer time horizon in mind. We also formed strategic partnerships across the state—working with grocery chains, warehouse developers, and property managers to install solar canopies and integrated energy systems that made financial and operational sense right away. That opened the door to larger, more predictable projects—and allowed us to reinvest in innovation.

Anna: You've also launched some innovative products under Vertical Solar Solutions. Can you tell me about the off-grid lighting system and what makes it unique?

Jim: Definitely. Our patented off-grid lighting system was designed to solve a specific problem: how do you deliver reliable, long-lasting lighting in places where trenching power lines is costly or impossible? Each unit uses bifacial solar panels, Li-ion battery storage, and high-performance LED light engines. They're rugged, self-contained, and built to operate for over a decade with zero maintenance. Cities love them for retrofitting, and commercial clients appreciate the operational savings and resilience.

Anna: They're also very stylish! What kind of clients are using these lighting systems?

Jim: We've deployed them across municipal projects, public parks, commercial properties, and remote industrial yards. Anywhere that needs dependable lighting without the cost and red tape of utility hook-ups. And because they're U.S.-made, they often qualify for additional tax incentives, which makes them even more attractive.

Anna: Let's talk about the Solar Time Tracker—this is such a smart way to maximize production. How did it come about?

Jim: Credit where it's due—the tracker itself was developed by Dennis Peet. We didn't create it, but we've chosen to use it for many of our installations because it solves a critical need: how to get more energy out of every panel without adding unnecessary complexity. The Solar Time Tracker uses a time-based rotation mechanism—no sensors, no GPS, no moving parts that can fail. It adjusts automatically throughout the day and resets at night, increasing production by up to 40% compared to fixed mounts. It's especially valuable for clients with open land who want better performance without the headaches of traditional tracking systems.

Anna: There are a few solar tracking systems on the market today—but yours clearly has some unique features. What sets it apart?

Jim: You're right—trackers aren't new, but most of them are overengineered and too maintenance-heavy for small- to mid-scale installs. What sets this one apart is the mounting system. It's built for simplicity, durability, and flexibility.

It's a single-post, time-based rotation system with no need for GPS or sensors that can drift or fail. The structure supports various panel types, and the mount is compact yet incredibly stable—perfect for rural properties, farms, and open commercial spaces.

There's no need for deep foundations or specialized equipment, which makes it much easier and more affordable to install—especially over uneven terrain. That's a huge win for customers who want tracking-level performance without the complexity of dual-axis systems.

Anna: Where is this type of tracker having the biggest impact?

Jim: It's incredibly versatile. We've installed them on farms, at wineries, over ponds—anywhere rooftop solar isn't ideal due to shading or structural limitations. The single-post design is stable in all kinds of weather and minimizes site disturbance, which helps keep project costs down. We're also seeing strong interest from rural homeowners. For folks with land but limited roof space, this is an elegant way to get the benefits of solar tracking without compromise. It's all about expanding access to efficient, high-performance solar—no matter where you live.

To Wrap It Up

Jim's journey is a powerful reminder that innovation is as much about timing as it is about vision. Anticipating what's next is critical—but so is listening to the market and staying agile enough to shift when needed. Beyond the tech, Jim is also leveraging strategic partnerships in steel and infrastructure to expand his footprint in new sectors.

His story (check out the full interview online) underscores a key message for every solar business leader: being first isn't always the win. As the *solar coaster* continues to twist and turn, knowing when to refocus and evolve are critical.

Up next, we'll explore one of the most unpredictable forces shaping our industry: policy. Because no matter how innovative your tech or how sharp your strategy, the regulatory environment can stall your momentum—or supercharge your success. Let's break down what's working, what's wavering, and what every solar company needs to watch closely.

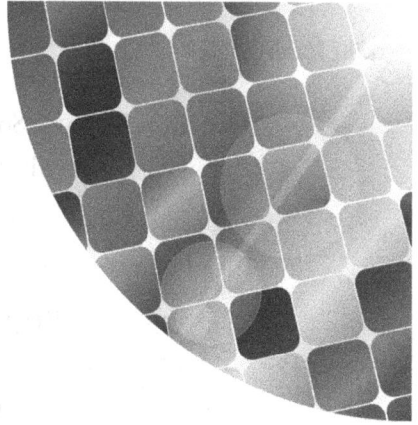

CHAPTER 8:

POLICY AND BEYOND

As we enter the final stretch of this book, it should be clearer what it takes to thrive in today's solar market. But if there's one thing we've learned, it's that what works today will be rewritten tomorrow. This chapter is about preparing you for what's next.

The future of solar depends on energy and carbon. More specifically, your role in reducing carbon emissions positions your business within the booming global carbon economy. This is where solar meets governance and how installation companies can evolve into impact-driven market leaders.

What is ESG—and Why Does it Matter in Solar?

ESG stands for Environmental, Social, and Governance—a framework used to measure how ethically and sustainably a company operates. It's no longer a niche concept. Investors, regulators, and even customers now use ESG scores to determine who they want to work with—and who they trust.

Here's where solar fits in:

- Environmental—Solar reduces carbon emissions and supports energy independence.

- Social—Solar improves community resilience, lowers bills, and boosts property value.

- Governance—Responsible companies monitor performance, honor warranties, and avoid greenwashing by backing up their claims with measurable impact.

Installing solar is a direct ESG accelerator, and your company is the one making that impact measurable.

Carbon Credits: A Monetizable Opportunity Hiding in Plain Sight

Carbon credits aren't just for Fortune 500s or utility-scale solar farms anymore. Today, even residential and commercial solar systems can tap into this global market. While most in the industry are familiar with SRECs or tax credits, carbon credits operate on a much larger scale— rewarding verified emissions reductions and unlocking new revenue streams that go beyond utility savings or state incentives. It's already being done.

Here's how it works:

1. Emission reduction projects (like solar, wind, reforestation) generate carbon credits.

2. Businesses buy those credits to offset their own emissions— because they have to (in regulated markets) or want to (in voluntary ESG efforts).

3. Credits are retired once used, locking in their impact—and freeing up demand for more.

Think of it like this: every kilowatt your system produces may hold more value than just the utility savings. It could soon come with a carbon-backed financial incentive—especially as policies tighten and demand increases globally.

There are two types of credits:

- Compliance credits (regulated by law; e.g., California Cap-and-Trade, EU ETS)

- Voluntary credits (used by companies like Delta and Shopify to meet sustainability goals)

This market is already moving, and solar companies are in prime position to benefit. The key is education, positioning, and partnerships that prepare you to capture that value.

> "Let's talk numbers. The global carbon credit market is expected to grow from $465 billion in 2023 to $3.1 trillion by 2030, with a staggering CAGR of 31.2%[10]. This is not a fringe trend. This is a tectonic shift in how global markets assign value to emissions, clean energy, and sustainability. And solar is at the center of it."
>
> – Jonathon Fletcher, VestSun

The Democratization of Clean Energy Ownership

Today, 77% of U.S. households are ineligible for rooftop solar due to rental status, shared roofs, structural issues, or aesthetic restrictions. On the commercial side, over 50% of properties are leased, making solar

---

10 https://www.businesswire.com/news/home/20250219311801/en/
Carbon-Credit-Global-Market-Outlook-2025-2030-with-Coverage-of-40-
Major-Players-including-3Degrees-CarbonBetter-ClearSky-Climate-Solutions-
Climate-Partner-Climeco-Climetrek-ForestCarbon-More---ResearchAndMarkets.
com

installation impractical for tenants—even those who want to meet ESG mandates.

But what if they could own a piece of the solution?

With blockchain-enabled solar ownership and fractionalized renewable assets, we're entering a future where renters, ESG-focused investors, and small businesses can buy into solar projects remotely—and earn carbon credits and long-term returns in the process.

Whether through developing solar farms, tokenizing energy credits, or aggregating community investments into RE-generating portfolios—the business models of tomorrow are forming today.

Policy Changes All The Time

Right now, solar companies across the country are bracing for the impact of the "One Big Beautiful Bill"—legislation that begins scaling back the 30% federal tax credit for residential solar starting after 2025, with tighter deadlines for commercial projects not far behind. If left unchallenged, these changes could erode the financial backbone of an industry that's powered America's clean energy transition for over a decade.

> *"We used to sell SunPower at 30% more than today's prices and still closed deals. If the tax credit disappears, we're right back there—selling premium solar with premium value. No panic. Just pivot."*
>
> – Damon Egglefield, Mirasol Solar

Smart solar players aren't waiting to change course. They're adapting—tightening operations, refining messaging, and leading with value instead of incentives.

And while the bill *can* be amended, that path runs through Congress—and it won't happen overnight. So in the meantime, the industry's best response is innovation.

From layered deal structures to EB-5 visa funding, energy-as-a-service models, and third-party ownership strategies, developers are proving that solar can still pencil—even when the policy doesn't. Which brings us to Alex Herrera, a developer who's rewriting the rules with unconventional funding and a strategic long game.

And finally, we'll hear from Ryan Park—a pioneer who's helped bring solar to the mainstream and is now building what's next with precision, purpose, and a deep understanding of the evolving market landscape.

CASE STUDY: FUNDING WITHOUT THE FLUFF: CREATIVE CAPITAL FOR CLEAN ENERGY

Like many of the leaders featured in this book, Alex Herrera didn't start where he ended up—and that's exactly what makes his story worth telling. When he first entered the solar industry, Alex believed the best path forward was residential solar with no credit score minimums—a mission rooted in accessibility and inclusion. But what he quickly discovered was that good intentions don't always align with good business models. The margins were thin. The risk exposure was high. And the long-term stability just wasn't there.

So, he pivoted. Alex turned his attention to commercial and utility-scale solar, where larger deals, long-term infrastructure, and experienced partners created a more sustainable path forward. And when it comes to funding?

Alex is not your average bear. He's built a reputation for using unconventional but strategic tools—like EB-5 "Gold Card" financing and layered deal structures—to get projects off the ground when others get stuck at the gate.

Sun Energy Today operates nationally, with a sharp focus on 10MW+ projects that serve high-impact sectors like public housing, school districts, resorts, data centers, airports, and municipalities.

Across all of those verticals, one thing unites his best clients: they want to save money, demonstrate sustainability, and ensure resiliency. But above all, they need to buy power. That's the core of it. Alex's job is to ensure there's a reliable off-taker on the other side of the meter—because when that piece is in place, everything else can be built around it.

Anna: Financing is often the make-or-break point for commercial solar. How do you approach structuring deals to keep them both bankable and flexible?"

Alex: It really depends on the deal. We use every tool in the box—cash, PPAs, traditional loans, and sometimes family offices, which are often attorney-backed private capital groups. But those deals usually come with strings attached—20% equity, and interest repayments.

Since they don't want the tax credits, we use them ourselves—and that's a huge advantage. We can monetize those credits and use the proceeds to pay down the loan and cover interest without giving up equity or control. It gives us more flexibility in how we finance and operate.

One of the more strategic tools in our toolbox—especially for community-serving solar—is EB-5 financing, or better known as the "Gold Card" program. It's a federal initiative that allows foreign investors to contribute $1 million to qualifying U.S. projects in exchange for a green card. Think of it like a low-interest, long-term government grant, but privately funded. The investors aren't looking for equity or a big payday. Their primary goal is immigration status. So, the repayment to the government is interest-only—you don't have to return the principal in the traditional sense. EB-5 is structured somewhat like a nonprofit; they can't capitalize on the investment itself, only on the interest income. That's what makes it so powerful—it lets us build at scale without stacking equity partners or taking on burdensome debt.

Now, to be clear, EB-5 only works in very specific scenarios. The project must serve the public good—such as public housing, schools, clean energy in low-income areas (or Opportunity Zones), workforce housing, or similar infrastructure that creates measurable community impact. EB-5 financing cannot be used for commercial resorts or private data centers. It's not about profit—it's about purpose.

Let me give you a hypothetical. If I could get Great Wolf Lodge to go solar—and they agreed to a power purchase agreement—I wouldn't fund that with family office money. I'd bring in EB-5. They'd provide the capital to build the system, and then Great Wolf would pay us monthly for the energy, just like they would with any utility. Meanwhile, EB-5 would be repaid via the interest on the loan, and we'd retain full control of the system.

But here's the catch: you need to work with a certified EB-5 representative to do it right. They handle the paperwork—engineering designs, financial models, job projections, community benefits—all the documentation that proves your project qualifies. The project either needs to be in a designated Opportunity Zone, or you need to demonstrate that it will create meaningful job growth and serve a disadvantaged community.

We're actively exploring EB-5 for solar farms that support public institutions—like school districts, public housing authorities, or nonprofits serving at-risk communities. When everything lines up, EB-5 is one of the most powerful and underutilized funding mechanisms in clean energy.

Anna: You mentioned being part of 48E and 45U—how do those incentives affect your project pipeline and long-term strategy?

Alex: They're a game-changer. These two provisions under the Inflation Reduction Act—48E and 45U—are reshaping the landscape for commercial solar and storage. 48E is the Investment Tax Credit (ITC) for clean energy projects, and it's replacing the old Section 48 ITC with new technology-neutral rules. 45U is the Production Tax Credit (PTC) version—it gives ongoing credits based on how much clean electricity you generate over time. The beautiful thing is, we can now pick which one works better financially for each project.

They both start strong, but they begin to phase down after 2031, which creates urgency—and filters out the noise. These programs are built for scale, not for small boutique installers. There's no official cutoff, but let's be honest: anything under 10 MW probably won't pencil out once you stack up interconnection costs, compliance, insurance, and all the engineering involved.

That's the biggest shift—we're seeing a clear market signal: *"If you're going to build clean energy, build it at scale."* And that's where we're already positioned. We're doing 50 MW, 100 MW, even 600 MW solar farms. We know how to get the financing, we know how to manage the stakeholders, and we know how to hit the deadlines before these tax credits taper off. Smaller players might not have the runway, or the relationships to make that happen.

So yes, 48E and 45U are huge. But they're not just tax credits. They're a competitive sorting mechanism, and the clock is already ticking.

Anna: So with credits like 25D, 30D, 30C, and 45V being eliminated—and transferability ending soon—how can the industry keep momentum without relying on incentives?

Alex: Let's be real—this is a stress test for the entire industry. These cuts, especially the EV infrastructure and hydrogen credits, hit newer sectors hard. A lot of companies built projections around those incentives. Now they're being told to recalculate.

But here's the thing—this always happens. Every few years, the rug shifts. That's why our team never chases short-term hype. We focus on infrastructure that will make sense even when the incentives fade.

The loss of transferability after 2026 is especially critical. That tool made it easier for smaller players to monetize tax credits without needing a tax equity investor. Without it, you'll see more consolidation. Fewer freelancers. And that's not all bad—it forces the industry to mature.

So how do we keep momentum?

1. Bank on fundamentals. Cheap power still wins. If you can sell clean electricity cheaper than the grid, you're still in business.

2. Build with partners who are in it for the long haul. Investors, landowners, off-takers—people who get the bigger picture.

3. Start creating hybrid values. We're combining solar, storage, EV infrastructure, and land-use deals like co-location with agriculture.

It's not about one credit or one product anymore—it's about layering value across sectors.

Honestly, this is a moment of clarification. The fluff is getting cut. The builders are staying. And if you've got a team that can think strategically, stack deals smartly, and find the value without relying on incentives—you're going to win. Not because of Washington. But because your business was built to last.

> "For safe-harboring commercial solar projects, until Treasury issues guidance, it's wise to consider purchasing assets equal to at least 5% of total project costs plus "turning dirt" (i.e. some physical work on the property). In addition, going higher than 5 percent is recommended to account for overruns and ensure you preserve full ITC eligibility."
>
> – Alan Schlissel, JD, MBA, LLM

Anna: You mentioned that you're exploring EV charging infrastructure. What's the opportunity there?

Alex: It's big—but still early. A Level 3 Supercharger setup costs around $100,000 installed, so incentives are critical. With the 30% federal credit—and an additional 10% bonus for low-income zones—these projects can make financial sense. But once those credits begin phasing out after 2031, a lot of the economics fall apart. Without that 30–40% upfront offset, your ROI stretches out fast—especially when you add permitting, interconnection, battery storage, and insurance.

We've explored large deployments like solar carports with integrated EV chargers at university campuses. The model works in high-traffic locations—you might buy power at $0.11/kWh and sell charging at $2.50 or more. But for lower-traffic sites, it doesn't pencil without incentives.

That's why this space is still in its infancy. The tech is advancing fast—especially with graphene-based supercapacitor batteries. These aren't your typical lithium systems. A supercapacitor fully charges in 15 minutes, discharges 100% of its stored energy, and can be recharged again almost instantly. Compare that to lithium, which discharges only about 70% and takes 90+ minutes to recharge once drained. That's a huge bottleneck in high-turnover locations.

With supercap batteries, we pull power from both the grid and the solar carport. The system is constantly feeding the EV charger, and once it's empty, it can be brought back online almost instantly. That kind of turnaround time is what makes the business model viable. It keeps the energy flowing and avoids long wait times for drivers—and more importantly, for revenue generation.

So yes, we're exploring it. The opportunity is real—but the economics are fragile. Without stable policy and long-term incentives, most projects won't survive the numbers. We're in—but we're moving cautiously and strategically, waiting for the market and regulations to mature.

Final Thoughts: When the Mission Meets the Math

If there's one thing Alex Herrera understands, it's that the solar industry is unpredictable. Incentives shift. Policies change. Projects stall. The only constant is uncertainty—and the people who thrive are the ones who stay flexible, think creatively, and lead with integrity.

As the founder of Sun Energy Today, Alex builds structures that can weather the ride. From commission-only deals to long-term ownership, from tax equity to EB-5 "Gold Card" financing, he has a rare talent for finding the model that fits, even when the landscape is shifting beneath his feet.

What we learned from Alex is this: there's always a way forward—if you're willing to get creative, stay grounded, and keep asking the right questions. Even if the tax credits vanish, even if the market shifts, the ones who know how to build with trust, clarity, and long-game vision will keep going.

Because on the solar coaster, it's not about avoiding the ups and downs. It's about learning how to ride. And no one rides it quite like Ryan Park.

While we've heard from pioneers, innovators, and industry builders throughout this book, Ryan's story brings it all home. He's been through the pivots, the policy changes, the booms, and the busts. He's sold inside Costco. He's built teams, opened markets, and seen the whole cycle unfold. But more than that, he's a reminder that the ones who own the future are the ones who learn from the past—and keep showing up for what's next.

Let's end with a mentor we can all learn from.

CASE STUDY: LESSONS FROM THE PAST, POWERING WHAT'S NEXT

Before I ever sat down to interview Ryan Park, I knew him as "the solar bachelor." Yes—*that* solar bachelor. Reality TV may have introduced him to a wider audience, but what most people don't know is that behind the screen-time charisma is one of the sharpest, fastest minds in solar.

Ryan lives just down the hill from me—so while we're not next-door neighbors, we're definitely in each other's orbit. We worked together on launching Powur in Hawaii and even sold a few systems side by side. Since then, we've built trust, swapped stories, and tackled some tough installs together. Over time, he's become a friend. But even more than that, he's become one of the people I turn to when I need clarity on the hardest questions in solar.

His depth of engineering knowledge is unmatched, and his ability to problem-solve in real time—especially around system design, expansion, and grid limitations—is nothing short of surgical. He sees around corners. He finds solutions when others throw in the towel. And he's lived through nearly every phase of the solar coaster: the startup hustle, the Costco wins, the rise of REC, the Sunrun acquisition, and the tough lessons from Duke Energy.

This isn't just a case study. It's a conversation with someone who's *been there, built it,* and is now shaping what comes next.

Anna: Ryan, where does your solar journey begin?

Ryan: I grew up in Fresno, California—track housing, smoggy summers where your lungs would burn from playing sports outside. I studied business at Cal Poly, and that's when I first started reading about solar. I realized I didn't just want to make money—I wanted to help improve the world too. One evening, I had dinner with a small group of student leaders and Paul Orfalea—who had just donated to name the Cal Poly College of Business after himself. I was lucky enough to sit right next to him. I sat next to him. He asked, "What business do you want to start?" I said, "Solar." He looked at me and said, "You're serious, huh? What are you doing Tuesday?"

He connected me with two business leaders in Santa Barbara—Tim Ball and Christine (Christy) Holz. They were early solar pioneers who had successfully built and sold a solar EPC (engineering, procurement, and construction) firm that specialized in off-grid systems for unique government applications. At the time, solar was still too expensive for mainstream adoption, but they believed the industry would grow exponentially as costs declined and technology improved.

I didn't know it at the time, but Tim and Christy had recently joined the Board of Directors for a small solar company in San Luis Obispo, founded by two Cal Poly alumni—Fred Sisson and Judy Ledford. They were mentoring the founders in exchange for equity, with the goal of helping the company grow into something meaningful.

When I met Tim and Christy and shared that I wanted to start a solar company, they invited me to prove myself. For several months, they gave me classic test assignments: If you had capital to start a solar company, what would you do? So I got to work—outlining sales strategies, analyzing competitors, sketching out team structures, and building a sample budget. Eventually, I presented it all. That's when Tim looked at me and asked, "Ryan, do you want to get your feet wet?"

My answer was a resounding yes.

He explained their role as board members for a small residential solar company run by Fred and Judy. "They're engineers," he said. "We've been helping them, but they need someone to drive revenue. Why don't you meet them? If they like you, you can lead the sales."

I met Fred, Judy, and Ethan Miller—a fellow recent Cal Poly grad who handled operations, including design engineering, procurement, and the (single) installation crew. I'll never forget that first meeting. The four of us squeezed into an office barely 500 square feet, with a tiny warehouse in the back. There was an instant connection, and I was all in.

The only challenge? The company was tiny and needed immediate revenue to stay afloat.

Fred told me, "We can start you at minimum wage, but we can't offer healthcare yet. However, if you can grow sales, we'll share 20% of the profit with you at year's end."

I said yes on the spot.

My parents, on the other hand, were full of hesitation. Why would I take a minimum-wage job at a startup with no benefits when consulting firms were offering stability, salary, and healthcare? But I knew where I belonged. At the time, the company was generating about $25,000 a month in revenue. Within six months, we were doing over $250,000 a month. I was obsessed—with solar, with selling, and with learning how to lead.

That was the launchpad. Scrappy, fast-paced, and foundational. And it changed everything.

Anna: What was it like in those early days?

Ryan: Back then, the company was called Renewable Energy Concepts. It was all hustle—guerrilla marketing, 1099 reps pounding the pavement, handing out flyers to promote solar education workshops at public libraries, and working 10x10 booths at home shows. We led with passion and talked about the bigger vision. There was no script, no playbook—just a deep belief that solar energy was the future.

As we expanded into small commercial installations, we began attracting early adopters—like family-owned wineries in Paso Robles. These owners weren't waiting for solar to be 20% cheaper than the electricity from fossil-fuel-burning power plants hundreds of miles away. They just wanted to know that a portion of their energy was coming from the sun—the same sun that ripened their grapes, without leaving behind smog or water pollution.

Everything was growing fast, but I realized I needed someone who could bring operational structure to our sales process—someone meticulous, but also able to rally people around a vision. It was time to make the biggest sale of my life: convincing my lifelong best friend and college roommate, Matthew Woods, to join the company.

At the time, Matthew was living the good life in Newport Beach, working as a rising sales professional at ADP, selling payroll services to small businesses. He was—and still is—a master of productivity and genuine persuasion, with a natural charisma that can't be taught. He had great pay, short workdays, and beachside weekends. Still, somehow, I convinced him to move back to San Luis Obispo for a few months to train with me before heading to Fresno to launch our Central Valley operation.

Matthew brought structure to the chaos. Together, we built a scalable sales system by adapting ADP's "7 Steps" framework for solar. It gave us rhythm, consistency, and results. We were building the plane while flying it—but it worked. We scaled fast, learned on the go, and made it happen without an advertising budget or a polished brand.

What set us apart was our culture. That was our X factor. Everyone on the team cared—deeply. About the mission, about the customers, and about doing the right thing even when it was hard. It wasn't perfect, but it was authentic. And it laid the foundation for everything that followed.

By 2006, we had momentum—but we also hit our first major challenge. Solar panel shortages and a flood of new competitors strained the market, and California's solar rebate funds were starting to run dry. We needed a strategic advantage—and leadership with experience beyond our youthful drive.

That's when Tim and Christy introduced us to Angiolo Laviziano, then CFO of Europe's largest solar installer, Conergy. Angiolo had helped take Conergy public, and they were looking to acquire a U.S. company to expand stateside. He spent a week with us in San Luis Obispo, interviewing and evaluating. In the end, Conergy made an offer to acquire us—but we declined.

To our surprise, Angiolo decided to leave Conergy and join us as CEO, investing his own money into the company. Yes, we gave up control—but it was a pivotal moment. We realized we had taken things as far as youthful energy and passion could go, and it was time for a seasoned leader who had been down this road before.

Under Angiolo's leadership, we rebranded from Renewable Energy Concepts to REC Solar. We also formed a new parent company—Mainstream Energy—to own and oversee REC Solar. As part of the growth strategy, we acquired AEE Solar, an established solar equipment distributor, to gain purchasing power and improve our cost structure.

It was critical, however, that each company operate independently. Installers wouldn't buy from AEE if they knew it was strengthening a direct competitor. So we kept the walls up, quietly fueling scale from behind the scenes.

Next, we launched a third company under Mainstream Energy: SnapNrack, which focused on developing faster, more efficient solar mounting solutions. REC Solar used SnapNrack products in the field, and AEE distributed them to other installers nationwide. Our business grew rapidly—and profitably—because we stayed frugal and got extraordinary productivity from our small but mighty team.

Still, we needed one more edge: better pricing on solar panels.

That's when another opportunity presented itself. In Europe, the solar boom was exploding. One major panel manufacturer in Norway—also named REC Solar—wanted to expand into the U.S. But we already owned the trademark here.

At the 2007 Solar Power International conference, the CEO of REC Solar Norway approached me to discuss the name conflict. When they learned we weren't just an installer, but also owned a major distribution company, the conversation shifted. We struck a deal.

REC Solar Norway invested $40 million into Mainstream Energy for a 20% stake—giving our company a $200 million valuation. The partnership also granted us exclusive rights to distribute REC Solar panels in the U.S.—securing our supply chain and giving us a significant strategic advantage with high-quality panels at unbeatable pricing.

It was a game-changing moment—and we were just getting started.

Anna: And then came Costco?

Ryan: It was massive. We didn't just land a contract to sell solar at Costco— we also secured the opportunity to install solar **on** Costco warehouses. The first installations rolled out in Hawaii, where we completed four rooftop systems, each just under 600 kW. That alone was a big win at the time. But what really changed the game was the second part of the deal.

Costco gave us a pilot opportunity to sell solar **inside** several of their retail stores—our choice of locations. At the time, we were only operating in California, but New Jersey was an emerging solar market we were eager to break into. So we chose three Costco stores in New Jersey to launch the in-store sales program.

The terms were simple: we had just a few weeks to hit a minimum sales threshold—or the program would be canceled. No one in the solar industry had ever sold through retail like this before. Failure wasn't an option. Fortunately, the timing aligned perfectly. New Jersey's Solar Renewable Energy Credit (SREC) program offered generous incentives that made solar a no-brainer financially. And the Costco model made it even easier— customers could buy pre-packaged 3, 6, or 9 kW systems using their Costco credit card.

I relocated to New Jersey and personally ran the first wave of in-store roadshows—40 straight days, open to close, standing solo at a Costco solar kiosk. No breaks. No team. Just me, a folding table, and a stream of curious customers.

Every morning, the roll-up doors came up and the store filled with people. I had to be sharp, fast, and dialed in. We were offering bundled systems—$9,000 for a 9 kW setup on a Costco card, with installation scheduled after a site survey. People were blown away. On the very first day, I gathered 53 qualified leads in just a few hours.

It was nonstop. We shattered sales records for every vendor Costco had ever worked with. And this was before solar leases were even a thing—people were paying out of pocket or using HELOCs. These were serious buyers.

I remember calling Angiolo and saying, "You've got to get someone out here now."

It was absolute chaos—in the best possible way.

Anna: Then came SolarCity and the invention of the residential lease?

Ryan: Yeah, that was wild. We actually met Lyndon Rive before SolarCity officially launched. Apparently, he and his brother Peter Rive—cousins of Elon Musk—first came up with the idea for SolarCity at Burning Man, of all places. They were dreaming big from the start. When Lyndon came through our office applying for a role to lead Northern California sales, we had no idea he was actually going undercover. He asked sharp questions—about our comp structure, our sales model, team size—and clearly knew the industry inside and out. He was overqualified, and of course, we offered him the job.

He declined.

Then he revealed the truth: he was about to become CEO of his own company—SolarCity—and in his words, they were going to eat our lunch. And to be honest? They kind of did.

When SolarCity arrived, they didn't just enter the market—they flooded it. With their zero-down offer and immediate 20–40% monthly savings off utility electricity prices, they flipped the industry on its head—and rewrote the rules of residential solar. They didn't just show up. They came to dominate.

Meanwhile, we were still selling systems through cash deals or HELOCs, saving customers 5–20% per month. It wasn't that our systems weren't better—it's just that their pitch was simpler, faster, and psychologically easier to say yes to. They made solar feel like cable TV: just sign here and save. But what most people didn't see was what was happening behind the curtain.

They'd sell a system at the installer contract level for around $5 a watt, then resell it to their own holding company at a valuation of $10 to $15 per watt. Why? To inflate the paper value of the project and claim massive tax credits based on those internal transfer prices. At that time, solar financial engineering was brand new, without clear IRS guidelines. It was a tax gray area—and it gave them fuel no one else had.

We were all scratching our heads—how are they offering systems this cheap? The truth was, they weren't playing by the same rules. They were playing the big picture. The margins weren't in the installs—they were buried in the finance stack.

It distorted the entire market. It set expectations that couldn't be met by companies trying to do it right. And it forced us to either adapt fast—or get run over.

Eventually, the tax rules were updated, and stricter guidelines were introduced to close that loophole and prevent inflated related-party valuations from skewing tax credit claims. But by then, the damage had been done. Investor expectations had already been warped. The bar had been set by smoke and mirrors—and honest operators were left to compete with the illusion.

That's when Lynn Jurich stepped in. A financial mastermind out of Stanford, she was one of the co-founders of what would become Sunrun. She already had the fund structured and ready to deploy. What she needed was a partner with real field operations—someone who could scale fast and execute cleanly.

We raised our hand and became Sunrun's first channel partner. That flipped the script. We finally had access to third-party ownership. We could offer the same zero-down simplicity—but with cleaner execution, ethical financing, and better tech behind it. It wasn't just about catching up—we were back in the fight, but this time doing it the right way.

And while SolarCity grabbed headlines, they're no longer around. Their model burned hot and fast, but it wasn't sustainable. They were top-heavy, burning cash, and not profitable—ever. Ultimately, SolarCity, billions in debt, was acquired by Tesla in a contentious bailout. These days, Tesla is the #1 battery storage provider in the U.S., and they are no longer in the business of installation—only equipment sales to installation companies like Sunrun.

Sunrun, on the other hand, evolved and endured—and we were right there in those early days, helping lay that foundation.

Anna: What about your exit to Sunrun?

Ryan: In 2012, Sunrun acquired REC's residential division. Technically, they purchased the REC Solar residential installation business, AEE Solar, and SnapNrack from Mainstream Energy, while REC Solar's commercial division remained separate. It was obviously a major milestone. Most of my close friends and executive teammates went to Sunrun—including Matthew Woods and Ethan Miller—but I didn't.

After supporting the New Jersey expansion with Costco, my heart was in commercial solar. I thrived on constantly learning, pushing limits, and deploying larger and more complex solar projects.

Looking back, before the deal with Sunrun happened, we were at a cross-roads. Inside the leadership circle, there was a serious debate. Some of us were pushing hard to create our own fund—to raise capital, own the financing, and truly control our growth. We knew that if we wanted to compete at scale, we couldn't keep relying on someone else's money. That was the move.

But Tim Ball—who added incredible value to our company with his wisdom over the years—disagreed. I'll never forget what he said: "Money is just a commodity. Our real value is in our execution and precision." And he meant it. He believed in craft, in delivering consistent quality, in staying lean and focused.

While he wasn't wrong about the importance of execution, he was completely wrong about where the true value would be recognized by the market at that stage of the industry. Looking back, that was the multi-billion dollar mistake. That was our moment to step up and own the capital stack. If we had trusted ourselves—if we'd taken that leap— we might've been the ones making acquisitions instead of being acquired.

Instead, we sold the residential business to Sunrun and spun off REC Commercial as its own company. I stayed on the commercial side—it was where I could keep building.

As for the Sunrun IPO? I was still a shareholder, but I was locked up when they went public. My investment advisors told me to diversify once the lock-up expired, so I sold early—right when the stock tanked during President Trump's first term, as he pushed to bring back coal. In my gut, I knew the stock was undervalued, but I didn't listen to my own advice. And sure enough, several years later, after I had sold most of my shares, it soared.

Sure, that stung—but honestly, the real regret wasn't the IPO timing. The real regret was not betting on ourselves sooner.

Execution matters. But in solar, capital is leverage. And we gave it away.

Anna: Where did things go from there?

Ryan: After the IPO, I stayed focused on commercial. We had momentum— solid projects, great teams, and we were finally getting traction at scale. One of the biggest early wins was landing a spot on the GSA Schedule, which let government agencies buy from us directly with pre-packaged system sizes, similar to what we did with Costco. That opened the door to major installs, like VA hospitals off the 405 in Santa Monica, CA. It was the kind of work we were built for.

But then came another painful lesson: those who control the finance stack, control the deals.

We landed a contract to solarize an entire school district in San Luis Obispo, where we remained headquartered. We partnered with SunEdison to provide the financing, as they would own and operate the solar projects after we installed them. We brought it in, did all the legwork, and after the ink was dry on the contract, SunEdison rewrote the specs—swapping us out of the installation for an out-of-town installer willing to build the projects for pennies of profit, or most likely, at a loss.

The deal collapsed. It felt like we got hustled. They played it like gangsters in suits—smiling through the handshake, then cutting us out. That moment was another clear signal: if you don't control the capital and the client, you're just a middleman. And middlemen don't get to make the rules.

That experience was a wake-up call—another reminder that without a steady funding partner and aligned execution, even the best projects can fall apart. We needed more control, more capital, and the ability to carry projects across the finish line without getting boxed out by shortsighted procurement games.

Not long after, Duke Energy came in and acquired REC Commercial. On paper, it looked like the right move. They had deep pockets, billions on the balance sheet, and access to cheap capital.

But in practice? It was a constant internal grind. Duke is a traditional utility company. They were so risk-averse it was paralyzing. If a potential client didn't have a Moody's rating or an investment-grade offtaker, it didn't move forward. Farmers? Small businesses? School districts? Community co-ops? Not "bankable." Never mind that they were ready, willing, and in desperate need of clean power.

We were trying to do it right—building real, bankable infrastructure that would last. But when your parent company won't fund anything without an investment-grade credit, even your best projects feel like you're running with a parachute strapped to your back. Eventually, the joy was gone. The mission got buried under risk reports and red tape.

So in 2016, I stepped away—not from solar, but from a version of it that no longer made sense. And honestly, that decision may have saved my love for the industry. Because now, I get to build again—with the lessons in hand, and a better view of where we need to go next.

Anna: Then what happened?

Ryan: After I left REC, I joined another startup to develop new racking technology for installing ground-mount solar without concrete piles, steel, or underground work—allowing projects to deploy quickly. We ballasted the racking with water. It was quite innovative and filled a good niche. We also figured out how to make solar panels a watertight roof for raised canopy structures. That solution was picked up by a large steel company, Nucor, which now markets the product as PowerShingle. That was a lot of fun. Looking back, we should have raised capital and scaled the company instead of handing the technology over.

When COVID hit, everything slowed down—but I didn't. I teamed up again with my longtime friend, Ethan Miller, who had run operations for REC Solar from the beginning. After the Sunrun acquisition, Ethan moved over and led national operations for them for many years.

Together, we started *Solar Shine*. It was one of those "let's fix something overlooked" ideas. Everyone tells homeowners to clean their panels, but most of the cleaning products out there either damage the panels or harm surrounding plants. Filthy solar panels don't let all the sunlight through, so electricity production can drop by 50% or more.

So we got to work—testing formulas, building prototypes, and designing something environmentally safe, effective, and scalable. It wasn't flashy, but it was real. And it felt good to be hands-on again. Why have solar panels on your roof if they aren't producing optimally?

That product is now available for sale on Amazon, and we plan to scale it. However, those plans were paused when Ethan was pulled back into operations—this time as COO of *Powur*, a fast-growing residential solar platform.

Powur combines direct-to-consumer sales with distributed installation, all managed through a centralized software platform. Think Amazon for home services—solar, roofing, storage, HVAC, and more. But unlike shipping a box, fulfilling solar involves local permits, regulations, and boots on the ground. Ethan was brought in to bring structure to that complexity.

I took notice. And when the opportunity came up to help expand Powur into Hawaii, I jumped in.

We moved to Honolulu over a decade ago—my wife is also in solar. She develops utility-scale projects and has deployed hundreds of megawatts across the islands. (Yes, we met at a solar conference.)

When Powur entered Hawaii—its 24th state—I helped with the launch and training of the local sales team. The sales came fast, but the usual challenges around engineering and execution remained. Fortunately, Powur had a key advantage: national equipment purchasing, which gave them better pricing than many local installers tied to distributor markups. I still support the team, provide mentorship, and occasionally take on projects for friends and family. In just two years, Powur has become one of the top solar companies in Hawaii.

Still, my passion for large-scale impact remained. That's when an opportunity came up to lead business development for the largest utility-scale Engineering, Procurement, and Construction (EPC) contractor in the U.S.—Moss & Associates.

Moss has built nearly 70% of all utility-scale solar and storage projects in Hawaii, including all the projects my wife developed in her role at Clearway Energy. Nationally, Moss is building multiple gigawatts of solar every year.

It's exciting to be part of a team making such a massive impact.

Anna: Knowing what you know now about solar—after riding the ups and downs, watching giants rise and fall—what do you think is coming next? And what advice would you give to solar business owners trying to survive what's ahead?

Ryan: First off—buckle up. This industry is not for the faint of heart. The volatility? It's not going anywhere. There will be political swings, regulatory uncertainty, and pressure from for-profit utilities defending the status quo. We're rebuilding the energy system in real time—while navigating shifting policies and unpredictable supply chain chaos.

So if you're here to ride a trend or flip a business, it's going to be brutal. But if you're here to build something that lasts—there's still enormous upside. Here's my advice: be smarter than we were the first time. Don't overextend. I've lived through the gold rush, the hype, the consolidation, and the implosions. What I've learned is this: smart execution beats fast growth every time. Build slow if you have to—but build right.

If possible, own your financing. Or partner with someone who will let you grow without pulling the rug out from under you. That was our billion-dollar mistake—we didn't create the fund when we should have. If you don't own the paper, you're just another sales org. You're expendable. Get on the capital side of the table.

Operationally, you have to be tighter than ever. Permitting, inspections, engineering—it's not optional to get this stuff right. Don't scale until your fulfillment machine is dialed. Trust me. I've seen what happens when it's not.

Stay ahead of tech. The landscape is changing fast. Microgrids and true energy independence are no longer futuristic—they're here. The opportunity is still massive. But this next chapter isn't about who can move the fastest—it's about who can move the smartest.

Wrap-Up: What Solar Business Owners Can Learn from Ryan Park

Ryan Park's journey is a clear reminder: control the capital, control the outcome. That means owning your financing—or partnering with those who align with your long-term vision. Without that, scale becomes risk, not reward.

Smart growth requires strong operations, clean fulfillment, and sharp policy awareness. Ryan's path shows that lasting success in solar comes from ownership, strategy, and a commitment to staying ahead of the curve.

CONCLUSION

A Night That Changed Everything

One of my most memorable nights happened in May 2022. My daughter's godmother was over to watch the sunset and share some pupus (AKA appetizers). The conversation shifted to the future—and my unwavering commitment to helping the world survive. She, of course, wanted to live, too, but she made it sound like none of it really mattered—like no matter what we did, the outcome was already decided. What could we do, really?

That night ended with me in tears—tears of pure passion for the fight ahead. I turned to her and said, *"It does matter, and I have to do something… What about Emma? When she talks about her future, what should I say? That she doesn't have one because we let fear, greed, and complacency dictate the fate of the world. Because no one stood up when it mattered most?"*

The truth is, I've wrestled with doubt—but I've never lost faith. The world is changing, and so are we. As conditions shift and innovation accelerates, I choose to believe that our efforts matter. Every step forward brings us closer to a greener, more sustainable future.

No matter what happens, I want to look my child in the eyes and say, *"I gave it everything I had."* So, she can grow up to be a singer, an interior designer, or whatever her heart desires—knowing that the world she dreams of is still within reach.

No matter what you believe in, let's agree on this: Our mission is to save the world. If you're reading this, you're now part of the story. You are more powerful than you realize, and I hope this gives you the momentum you need to keep going—to push forward, to think bigger, to be bolder.

We are lucky enough to be part of the most significant energy transformation in human history. This is an evolutionary leap, and we are the ones carrying the torch.

The Future is Now—And it's Electrifying

I'm excited by the wave of next-level innovations reshaping entire industries. Companies like Altitude Water are pulling clean water straight from the atmosphere, turning air into a life-sustaining resource. Hydrogen pioneers are redefining what's possible in transportation and energy storage. Next-gen recycling and biofuels are turning waste into power. Advanced nuclear energy is evolving, offering cleaner, more scalable power. And within our homes, AI-driven systems are eliminating waste and optimizing efficiency—silently improving our lives behind the scenes.

One of the biggest game-changers is happening right in front of us: solar automation. At InterSolar 2025, installer robots were unveiled—not to replace humans, but to empower them. These machines are our superpower sidekicks—cutting costs, accelerating installations, and unlocking massive opportunity across the solar ecosystem. From business owners and manufacturers to financiers, installers, and consultants, everyone benefits when we raise the bar together. Pair that with the explosive growth in building-integrated solar design, and we're witnessing a total reinvention of how we power and shape the world. Companies like GAF are leading the charge with durable, fire-rated shingles that generate energy and come backed by 50-year warranties. Eco-efficiency isn't the future. It's right now. But let's be honest: we're also at a crossroads. Economic pressures, policy uncertainty, and rising consumer hesitation are testing every part of this industry. We've been here before.

There was a time when solar had no tax credits. We still showed up. We still sold. We still built.

Those incentives were never guaranteed—and we always knew they'd end someday.

Maybe they'll come back. Maybe they won't.

But no matter what Congress decides—or how the markets swing— we don't wait for permission. We lead. Now.

As our energy-driven world keeps evolving, I hope you—solar heroes—will be standing right there with me, at the front lines, pushing forward. Connecting with one another. Sharing resources. Learning fast. And driving meaningful change—together.

Because the truth is: we can't build the future alone.

When I was just getting started in solar, I found myself in rooms filled with giants—agencies representing dozens of dealers, while I had only two. I debated offering exclusivity in certain territories—limiting myself to one dealer per market, similar to the Master Dealer model. I'll never forget Kelley Barber's advice: *"There are enough homes for everyone."* She was right. That one insight changed everything for me.

Instead of limiting growth, I leaned into collaboration. I realized that having multiple dealers in a single market could actually strengthen performance—boosting media leverage, giving us more control in the lead exchange, and lowering cost per click. The more of them there were, the stronger we all became.

And through it all, Kelley had my back. Even as leadership changed hands at her company, she showed unwavering loyalty—speaking up for me in rooms I wasn't in, making sure people knew the value we were bringing. That kind of integrity is rare—and exactly what this industry needs more of right now, so if you take one thing with you from this book, let it be this: we are stronger when we build together.

And one of the best ways to keep building is by staying connected. If you're looking for more case studies, resources, behind-the-scenes insights, and expert interviews, visit SolarCoasterBook.com and subscribe to The Solar Coaster Podcast to stay current on all the juicy industry gossip—and reach out to be a guest!

The solar industry is evolving. Innovation, adaptability, and strategic expansion will define the winners in the years ahead. But what if we, as an industry, took it a step further? With a record number of billionaires today and the sour taste of solar tax credits being put on ice, could we band together to create a self-sustaining fund to drive the next wave of clean energy adoption? Instead of waiting for policy shifts, what if we became the architects of our own green future?

The opportunity is here. The power is in our hands. So, let's sell some kWs and change the world!

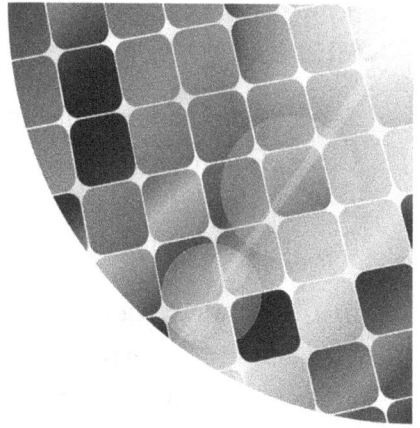

ABOUT THE AUTHOR

Anna Covert is a highly successful solar entrepreneur and a passionate advocate for the solar industry. She is an innovator who has designed numerous technology solutions and products that solve problems for solar consumers and business owners as they engage online and offline.

Anna is also the founder and principal of Covert Communication, the largest digital marketing firm in Hawaii. An expert in advertising and marketing, she has worked with hundreds of companies worldwide on both the client and agency side, providing strategic consulting to Fortune 500 companies and fusing her traditional and online media experience into a unique and seamless approach to building next-generation marketing strategies.

Anna is a Forbes Author of the bestseller *The Covert Code - Mastering The Art Of Digital Marketing* and host of the popular *The Covert Code* podcast - thecovertcode.com

Services that Anna and her companies provide are:

Covert Communication – Integrated Marketing. Helping brands extend their traditional marketing efforts online, providing innovative, results-driven, integrated digital solutions.

Trusting Solar Calculator (Solar Wizard) – Solar calculator app that provides estimates of solar costs and savings for residential and commercial companies. Completely customizable, multi-languages, currently being used in over 27 countries.

Aerial Impacts – Customized direct mail company focused on home services to provide customized variable printed postcards to homeowners showing their home with solar on the roof.

Solar Assault – A high-impact direct mail campaign using variable printing and personalized messaging to reach prospects along the sales funnel and drive conversions with custom offers and localized visuals.

Reactium.io – A powerful open-source web platform providing full-stack technology services.

MANA – Software to save time and money. In Hawaiian MANA means power. The mission is to connect application programming interfaces through custom code without the use of Zapier or third-party services.

Anna can be reached at anna@covertcommunication.com, on LinkedIn, or through any of her websites, including AnnaCovert.com, for public speaking engagements.

www.ingramcontent.com/pod-product-compliance
Lightning Source LLC
Chambersburg PA
CBHW072306210326
41519CB00057B/2815